EMBROIDER YOUR LIFE

TECHNIQUES + MOTIFS + INSPIRATION

Simple TECHNIQUES & 150 Stylish MOTIFS TO EMBELLISH YOUR WORLD

NATHALIE MORNU

ALPHA

CONTENTS

MATERIALS, TOOLS & TECHNIQUES

COTTON FLOSS
This is what people typically think of as embroidery floss. The hank usually has six strands loosely twisted together. You can stitch with anywhere from one to six strands—just separate them. Floss comes in literally hundreds of colors.

CREWEL WOOL
This wool yarn gives embroidery a warm texture.

PERLE COTTON
This has a lovely beaded texture that looks terrific in embroidery. Size 12 (shown) is a heavier weight than sizes 8 and 5 (see below), and comes in hanks.

YARN
Use any super fine yarn (labeled with a yarn weight of 1).

FLOSS & THREAD

You can use any fiber that you're able to thread on a needle, so long as its thickness doesn't cause the fabric to pucker around it.

SILK FLOSS
This thread has a glossy appearance.

BAKER'S TWINE
This rope-like thread is usually two-tone.

SEWING THREAD
Any type works, cotton or polyester.

PERLE COTTON
Size 5 is a fine strand sold in balls.

METALLIC FLOSS
Comes in many shimmery shades.

CROCHET THREAD
This laceweight yarn is labeled yarn weight 0.

Floss Bobbins
Storing floss on a plastic or cardboard bobbin prevents it from tangling. Simply wind one thread color neatly around the bobbin—it only takes a minute—and catch the end in the slit so it doesn't unwind.

PLASTIC HOOP
This type is the one most commonly sold in craft stores. It does only a fair job of holding fabric taut.

HOOPS

Hoops hold your fabric taut so that you can embroider the motif more easily. They come in a range of sizes. Using a smaller hoop is easier, but it may require shifting the fabric and motif more frequently.

BENTWOOD HOOPS
These grip fabric tighly. Buy the high-quality, expensive type; you're likely to find them only online. The cheap ones sold in craft stores won't hold the fabric taut enough.

BRASS HOOP
This new hoop design holds the fabric between a coil and a channel in the ring. It's best suited for lightweight fabrics.

SPRING TENSION HOOP
Although these are designed for machine embroidery, they work well for hand embroidery, too.

OVAL HOOP
Bentwood hoops come in oval, round, and square. What shape you use doesn't matter–it's just a matter of preference. You may need a small screwdriver to tighten the screw.

Embroidery shows up best on solid colors and fabrics with smooth surfaces.

FABRIC

Fabric is the foundation on which you draw with thread. The looser its weave, the easier it will be to pull the needle and floss through, and therefore the easier to embroider on.

CHOOSING FABRIC

You can embroider on any cloth short of tulle (the netting on tutus) and fabrics with pile, like velvet and corduroy. That's because tulle is more air than fiber, and because embroidery stitches will get buried in the short, projecting threads of the velvet pile and become invisible. Select a fabric that can support the weight of your stitches. Heavy thread will cause lightweight cloth like lawn to pucker around it, while light thread work on heavy material like upholstery fabric or canvas may barely appear visible.

WASH FABRIC BEFORE USE

New fabrics are treated with a product that keeps them looking crisp on the bolt. You don't want that chemical in your embroidery because it breaks down fibers over time. New fabrics may also shrink when washed. It's heartbreaking to spend all that time embroidering, then wash the embroidery later only to find it ruined because the foundation fabric shrunk. So wash all new fabrics before you embroider, to pre-shrink them and remove all chemicals. It's fine to put cotton in the dryer, but hang wool and linen on a line to dry.

FABRIC TYPES

Any fabric without pile (soft threads pointing up, like on velvet) is fair game as a surface for embroidery.

Linen. For centuries, embroidery was traditionally stitched on linen—which is made from the flax plant—partly because it was one of the earliest woven fabrics and easier to grow than cotton, and partly for its durability, crispness, lovely drape, and the cool feel of it in the hand. Linen production is labor-intensive, making it a pricy fabric.

Cotton. Cotton fabric is popular for embroidery because it's inexpensive, easy to source, and comes in a rainbow of shades as well as prints, which you can embroider on as long as you select a thick enough floss in a color that stands out.

Wool and felt. Wool has a wonderfully rich feel, and looks very lush when embroidered with wool crewel yarn. Felt is a non-woven wool fabric. With its fuzziness and association with childhood, it lends a playful feel to crafts, which may be why it's so popular for embroidered patches. The felt sold in most craft stores is polyester with a patchy thickness that looks cheap and tears easily. Try to find wool or wool blends instead.

Knits. Yes, you can embroider on stretchy fabrics, which range from jersey (the fabric used to make T-shirts) to fine-weight sweaters. You simply need to back the stitched area with a stabilizer to prevent the stitching from distorting.

Denim. Really, what's cooler than flower-embroidered hippie-girl jeans or a denim jacket? Denim is the perfect canvas for embroidery because it's neutral and it looks even better with age.

Existing garments. Don't feel that you have to buy fabric off a bolt. You can snip fabric off old apparel—just avoid stained areas—or embroider a section of a piece of clothing.

NEEDLES

There are many different specialty needles, and any of them will work for embroidery. Don't get too bogged down about specifically using embroidery needles. You'll need a small upholstery needle when stitching with yarn.

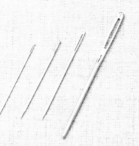

SEAM RIPPER

This tool can be useful for removing stitches, but be very gentle while using it, or you'll damage the fabric.

NEEDLE THREADER

Essential for threading heavy fibers! To use it, first slip the wire loop through the eye of your needle, then pass the end of your thread into the wire loop. End by gently pulling the threader out of the eye, pulling the thread through the eye as you do.

OTHER TOOLS

You'll find some of these tools in the notions department of your fabric store, while others are stocked in the quilting section. Craft stores stock interfacing and stabilizer with the fabrics.

THIMBLE

Helps you push the needle through heavy material like denim. Not essential for lightweight fabrics.

FABRIC SHEARS

Reserve these for cutting cloth, and have them regularly sharpened by a professional. Keep a separate pair of scissors for paper, which dulls blades.

PINS

Use these to hold the paper or tear-away stabilizer with your motif on it against the fabric.

EMBROIDERY SCISSORS

Short, sharp blades allow you to get into tight spaces to snip thread. Reserve these only for cutting thread–nothing else.

DOUBLE-STICK TAPE

Keeps your finished embroidery taut on a mat board when mounting it.

TEAR-AWAY STABILIZER

With its perforations, this material is designed to tear easily. You'll use it for transferring motifs.

LIGHTWEIGHT FUSIBLE INTERFACING

Use one-sided interfacing as a stabilizer. Purchase the lightest weight possible. Double-sided interfacing is for appliqués.

WATER-SOLUBLE STABILIZER

Use it for transferring motifs. It melts away in water when you no longer need it.

HOT IRON TRANFER PENCIL

If you draw a motif with this pencil and iron over the back of it, it transfers to another surface.

TRANSFER PAPER

Comes in five colors to transfer motifs on every shade of fabric. Avoid applying pressure anywhere but on the motif; otherwise, you'll leave behind smudges on the fabric.

WATER-SOLUBLE PEN

A line drawn with this pen disappears every time when you lightly dab water on it with a cotton swab—no fuss, no need to scrub.

IRON-OFF MARKER

Use for transferring motifs onto dark fabrics. If the ink doesn't show up immediately, give it a moment. When you no longer need it, it vanishes when you pass a hot iron over it.

WATER-SOLUBLE PENCILS

Between them, blue and white pencils can mark every color of fabric. Be sure to test that it comes off by trying it on a corner of the fabric before use.

SOAPSTONE MARKER

Perfect for transferring motifs onto dark fabrics. It simply rubs off.

WATER-SOLUBLE GRAPHITE PENCIL

Only for light-colored fabrics. Press as lightly as possible. The graphite may require mild soap to remove.

HOW TO PLACE THE FABRIC IN THE HOOP

1. Loosen the screw on the outer ring of the hoop. Separate the rings and set aside the outer one.

2. Put the inner ring on a flat work surface. Place the fabric face up over it, centering the motif (or the part of the motif you want to stitch) on it.

3. Push the outer ring onto the inner one; if it doesn't fit, loosen the screw until it does. While gently and evenly pulling the fabric taut, tighten the screw until the hoop holds the fabric tightly.

This shows the back of the fabric after you've placed it in the hoop

FABRIC

Try to leave at least 3 inches (10cm) of cloth around the motif when you draw it. This gives you enough fabric to catch it in the hoop and embroider, and plenty of options for what to do with the finished item–framing it or sewing it to something else, for example.

STABILIZER

Stabilizer prevents knit fabrics from stretching and adds an opaque layer that keeps stitches on the back from showing through thin fabrics. Traditionally, embroiderers use non-stretch fabric like cotton or muslin as stabilizer, cutting it to the same size as the foundation fabric and basting it on the wrong side of the fabric. Since it's unwieldy to work with several layers of cloth, a simpler option is to instead attach one-sided fusible interfacing as follows, before placing the fabric in the hoop.

1. Transfer the motif onto the right side of the fabric.

2. Cut a square of fusible interfacing a bit larger than the motif (or, if desired, the size of the foundation fabric).

3. Turn on your iron and place the fabric right side down on the ironing board.

4. Feel both sides of the fusible interfacing. Only one side has little bumps. The bumps are an adhesive that melts under heat. Place the side with the bumps face down against the fabric, directly behind the motif. (This is important! If you place the bumps face up, the interfacing will stick to the iron, and you'll have to scrape it all off after the iron cools.) Check again. Are the bumps face down? If so, pass the iron gently over the interfacing to adhere it to the fabric.

GETTING STARTED

Embroidery is a simple technique. You merely follow the lines of the motif with your needle and thread, or fill areas with stitches. These techniques and tips will ensure your success.

- Transfer the motif onto the fabric first, leaving enough fabric around it to place it in the hoop later.

- Embroider with clean hands that are free of lotion. Hand creams can stain fabric and thread.

- There should be no food or drink on your work surface. They can stain fabric or cause the motif to vanish before you've finished embroidering it.

- Make sure the fabric is taut, like a drum, in the hoop. It may loosen over time. This makes embroidering a little trickier: the motif is harder to see, the thread snags or tangles, and stitching is harder. When the cloth loosens, simply tug it gently from below the hoop, pulling all around so the fabric doesn't get distorted. Then further tighten the screw.

- Always work with good light. It's easy to mistake thread colors in dim conditions.

- After you finish embroidering, remove any visible lines from the motif, then carefully iron using the steam setting.

- Owning several hoops allows you to have several pieces going at once, which can stave off boredom on long projects–just switch from one to another.

Definition

BASTING
The act of temporarily holding two pieces of fabric together using long stitches of $^1/_2$ inch (1.3cm) or more.

Definition

RIGHT SIDE AND WRONG SIDE OF FABRIC
The side printed with color or pattern is the right side. The other one is called the wrong side. For cotton or linen that looks the same on both sides, either side is the right side.

No-Slip Hoop
This plastic hoop has a channel in it that, when the hoop is tight, catches the fabric more tightly than hoops with flat sides. Fabric mounted in this type of hoop stays taut much longer.

TRANSFERRING MOTIFS

You can find motifs literally anywhere. Practically any image can be embroidered. After assembling your materials and tools and selecting a motif, you need to get it onto your fabric so that you can embroider it.

Don't feel obligated to use motifs designed specifically for embroidery. You can find designs anywhere and everywhere. Just look for any imagery you like online, in print, on T-shirts, in kids' drawings, on posters–the list of options could on and on. The imagery doesn't have to start out as an illustration. You might trace the outline of an object in a photograph you've taken, for example. As a final note, feel free to add to your motif, crop out any part of the drawing that you don't want, or mash up several images. This is your embroidery, so customize it!

1 Make a copy of the motif first

If your original image is in a book or on some other physical object, rather than from a digital source, you should avoid drawing directly on the original. Pen marks all over it will degrade its quality and you won't have a clear original if you want to reuse it again later as a motif. Simply make a photocopy of the motif, or scan it and print it.

If you don't have access to a photocopier, just take a snapshot of the image, transfer it to your computer, and print it. No computer? Just trace the design onto tracing paper.

2 Resize the motif if desired

You've selected your motif, but perhaps it doesn't feel like it's the right size. That's absolutely no problem–you can easily make it larger or smaller.

Most photocopiers have an enlarge/reduce option. Position your original (or the copy) on the glass, and choose the percentage you want to copy it at. (Any number under 100% will reduce it; over 100% enlarges it. For example, 50% will make it half its original size, while 200% doubles it.) Check the copy. If you like what you see, great. If not, try a different number to get a different size.

3 Choose a transfer method

This book explains five different transfer methods. Why? To give you options. Some methods don't work on dark fabrics. Others require some special supplies that you might not have on hand, necessitating a trip to the fabric store. The window transfer method is the simplest and needs only materials that you're almost certain to have on hand, but it can't be done at night. Each method includes a box with an exclamtion point icon inside it, listing pros and cons. Compare these points against your fabric and materials, then choose your method accordingly.

It's generally best to transfer the motif onto the right side of the fabric. That's because you want to stitch right onto the design, and that's why you use pens and pencils with disappearing pigment that you can remove after you stitch. Following a pattern that you've placed on the back of the fabric but stitching on the front may result in distortion of the motif.

Never, ever use an ink pen to draw a motif on fabric. If you wash the embroidered item later, the ink will bleed on the fabric and ruin the stitching.

WINDOW TRANSFER

This method works only for light- to medium-weight fabrics, because you can't see through heavy material. It can be slightly more challenging, but still possible, on dark fabrics. It requires a sunny day—the sunnier, the better—so plan ahead if you wish to stitch in the evening.

 Requires daylight; no special tools needed; not for heavy or fuzzy fabrics, nor for really dark colors.

What you'll need
Sheet of paper containing the motif
Tape
Fabric
Pins
Any kind of transfer pen or pencil

This technique always works with a lightbox, no matter the time or cloudiness of the day.

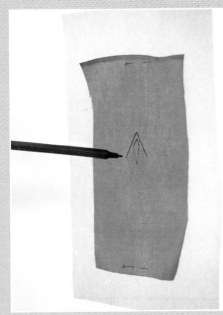

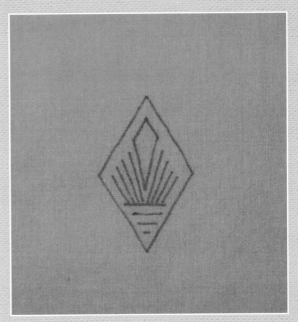

1 TAPE AGAINST WINDOW
If the motif is light, darken it by going over it with a black ink pen. Then tape the four corners of the paper containing the motif to your window, with the motif face up. Place the fabric face up against the motif, and pin the top and bottom to the paper. Begin tracing ...

2 TRACE UNTIL FINISHED
After tracing, don't immediately unpin the fabric. Instead, unpin just the bottom. Lift up the fabric and compare the original motif to the one on the fabric to make sure you transferred every line. (Keeping the top of the fabric pinned to the paper will make it easier to line up both images if you missed anything and need to continue tracing.) Once you're satisfied that you've transferred every line, unpin the fabric and untape the paper.

TEAR-AWAY STABILIZER

This is the best transfer method for embroidering on dark fabric, and it works equally well on all colors. It does require extra time, after you tear it off, to pick away all the little pieces of stabilizer stuck in corners and under dense stitching.

> ❗ Requires specialized stabilizer; ideal for all fabric colors, weights, and types.

What you'll need

Motif	Embroidery hoop
Tear-away stabilizer	Pins
Ink pen	Needle and floss
Fabric	Embroidery scissors

Use a pin to gently scratch away bits of stabilizer caught under the stitching and in tight corners.

Keeping the fabric taut in the hoop makes it easier to tear away the stabilizer.

Leave the stabilizer out of the hoop so the hoop grips the same thickness of fabric all around.

1 PIN ON THE STABILIZER & STITCH
Transfer the motif onto the tear-away stabilizer using the window method, or any other you prefer. Place your fabric in the hoop, then pin the stabilizer tautly to it with the motif face up. Embroider the entire motif, stitching directly on the stabilizer.

2 TEAR AWAY THE STABILIZER
Leaving the fabric in the hoop, remove all the pins. Tear away the stabilizer from the exterior of the embroidered motif first, working gently to avoid damaging the stitching. Then pick away the tear-away stabilizer from the inside of the motif.

HOT IRON TRANSFER PENCIL

This method is direct and immediate, and therefore feels simple to do. It's not suitable for dark-colored fabrics, however, as the transfer it leaves behind is fairly faint.

 Reverses the motif; requires specialized tool; for light fabric colors only; not for fuzzy fabrics.

What you'll need
Blank sheet of paper
Motif
Hot iron transfer pencil
Fabric
Iron and ironing board

This transfer is permanent, so you must cover it completely with embroidery.

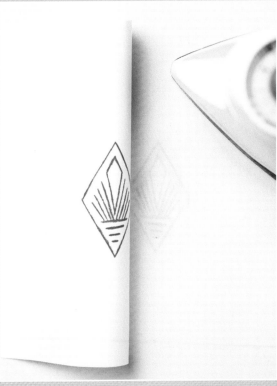

1 DRAW THE MOTIF
Place the blank sheet of paper over your motif, and trace over it using the hot iron transfer pencil. (If you can't see through the top sheet of paper, place both on a window). As you trace, press firmly. The harder you press, the better the motif will transfer in the next step.

Keep the motif oriented correctly
This method transfers the design backward. If the motif includes words or numbers, or has a definite left and right, you must start step 2 with a reverse image. To achieve this, begin by placing the motif against a window with the design face down. It should read backward through the paper. Trace the reverse image onto the back of the paper with the hot iron transfer pencil.

2 IRON IT ONTO THE FABRIC
Turn on the iron to maximum heat ,with the steam turned off. (Or pour out any water.) Put the fabric face up on the ironing board. Place the paper with the motif drawn in hot-iron transfer pencil face down on the fabric. While holding the paper securely in place with your fingers, press firmly with the hot iron for at least five seconds.

TRANSFER PAPER

Transfer paper is pricey, but comes in five colors so you're sure to find a shade that shows up on any color cloth. Carbon paper from office supply stores is cheaper and works well–but only comes in black and won't be visible on dark fabric.

 Requires specialized transfer paper; for all fabric colors; not for fuzzy fabrics like felt.

What you'll need
Fabric
Transfer paper
Sheet of paper containing the motif
Ballpoint pen

Use a pen in a different color from the motif so you can see what you've already traced.

To avoid leaving smudges on the fabric, cut the transfer paper just larger than the motif.

1 STACK THE MATERIALS
Work on a soft surface like a thick magazine. (This allows your pen to dig deeper and transfer more carbon.) Lay the fabric face up. Put the transfer paper face down on the fabric. Place the paper with the motif face up on top. Hold the paper with your fingertips, applying as little pressure as possible to avoid leaving smudges on the fabric. Begin tracing, applying firm pressure ...

2 TRACE UNTIL FINISHED
After tracing, don't remove the sheets of paper from the fabric immediately. Instead, still applying as little pressure as possible, hold the layers in place but pull just a corner of the transfer paper back to check that the motif is visible enough. If not, trace again, applying still more pressure.

ADHESIVE WATER-SOLUBLE STABILIZER

This method works for transferring a motif onto any shade of fabric. The adhesive type of stabilizer used here has a cool feature: the backing stiffens it, so you can run it through a printer–which allows you to print any motif onto it from your computer.

! Requires specialized stabilizer; for all fabric colors, weights, and types.

What you'll need
Motif
Adhesive water-soluble stabilizer*
Any marking device except ink pen**
Scissors
Fabric
Embroidery hoop
Needle and floss
Bowl of water and a sink

*If you can't find the adhesive kind, use the nonadhesive type. You'll simply have to baste it on.

**Ink will stain the fabric when you wash away the stabilizer in step 2.

Soaking for an hour or more and then rinsing helps the product wash away properly.

Cutting off extra stabilizer means there's less to remove later.

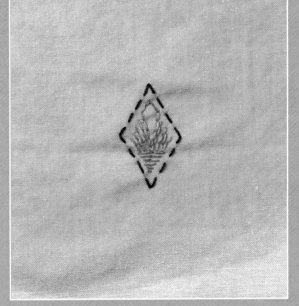

1 ADHERE THE STABILIZER & STITCH
If desired, print the motif from your computer onto the water-soluble stabilizer. Otherwise, place the water-soluble stabilizer over the motif, rough side up, and trace it. Place the fabric in the hoop. Cut out the motif near the edge, then peel away the adhesive backing and adhere the stabilizer to the fabric. (If using nonadhesive stabilizer, leave about 2 inches [5cm] all around the motif and either pin or baste the stabilizer to the fabric.) Finally, embroider the entire design.

2 SOAK & RINSE
Dunk the fabric into a bowl of lukewarm water and let it soak for at least an hour, then rinse it gently under running water. Roll the embroidery in a towel to blot out most of the water, then remove the fabric and let it air dry. If it feels stiff afterward, you didn't get all the product out; just soak and rinse it again.

WORKING WITH FLOSS

These pointers and techniques will help you keep your floss under control.

Thread conditioner

EMBROIDERY Q&A

- **HOW LONG OF A THREAD SHOULD I STITCH WITH?** Use only as much as you can manage. Beginners should stick to 24 inches (61cm) so it doesn't tangle and snarl, but experienced stitchers can go with more.

- **HOW MANY STRANDS CAN I USE?** There's no rule. You may stitch with all six strands of cotton floss, or separate off fewer. You can double a single strand of perle cotton or crochet thread, but more than one strand of crewel yarn or yarn will twist and look messy.

- **SHOULD I CONDITION THREAD?** Thread conditioner is optional, but helps prevent tangling and fraying. Simply run the floss once through the product before threading it onto the needle. Don't use thread conditioner on yarn.

- **HOW DO I SEPARATE STRANDS OF COTTON FLOSS?** Use one hand to grasp the desired number of strands at the end of the cut piece, and hold the rest in the other. Letting the strands dangle, gently pull them apart bit by bit, allowing them to slowly untwist. Tugging will result in a snarl.

HOW TO START THREAD

Knots create lumps on the back of the embroidery. To avoid this, start all threads with a waste knot, as follows.

The waste knot is on the front, away from the motif.

front

1 Knot the thread on a threaded needle. Bring the needle through the front of the fabric, at least 3 inches (7.5cm) away from where you wish to embroider.

2 Embroider the entire motif. Afterward, you'll snip the thread immediately next to all waste knots and pull the threads through to the back. Fasten off, following the instructions on the next page.

HOW TO CARRY THREAD

Carrying simply means to jump from one area to another.

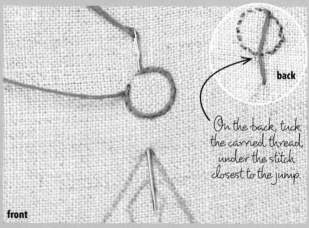

back

On the back, tuck the carried thread under the stitch closest to the jump.

front

When you finish stitching one area of a motif, you can either fasten off the thread or take the needle to another section, working on the back of the fabric. Carrying is more efficient, time-wise. Try to carry thread for the shortest distance possible—no more than 1 inch (2.5cm). Long carried threads can create looseness in the stitches showing on the front, or puckers in the fabric.

- **SHOULD I TIE KNOTS?** Traditional embroidery has no knots to keep it looking as good on the back as on the front, but don't get too hung up on that rule. A single knot tied at the end of a piece of thread is usually quite small and may pop through the fabric. So just tie several knots on top of each other.

- **WHERE DO I START STITCHING?** It absolutely doesn't matter.

- **WHAT DIRECTION DO I STITCH?** Again, it doesn't matter.

- **WHEN CAN I TAKE A BREAK?** Stop anytime. If you still have thread left on the needle, "park" it through two stitches, either on the front or the back. Leaving it poked through the fabric for long can permanently distort the cloth's fibers.

- **MY FLOSS LOOKS TATTERED—NOW WHAT?** Replace the floss the moment it gets raggedy, or your embroidery will look scraggly.

TIPS FOR SUCCESS

THREAD AHEAD Threading new thread in the middle of a project interrupts the fun of the stitching. This may tempt you to keep using ragged-looking thread. To thwart this inclination, thread three needles with each color of floss before starting.

EMBROIDERING ON PRINTED FABRICS To ensure the embroidery shows, choose bright colors of thread that contrast with the fabric, and use more strands to create a thicker line.

TEST FLOSS FOR COLOR-FASTNESS Floss is supposed to be color-fast, but sometimes that promise doesn't hold. Always test your floss before you embroider with it to make sure the dye won't run. To do this, stitch about 6 inches (15cm) of long running stitches on some fabric. Soak it in warm water. If the stitches bleed, toss the floss.

HOW TO FASTEN OFF

Fasten off when you have less than 4 inches (10cm) of thread left on the needle or when it looks scraggly.

back

Working thread

1 Working on the back, skip the two stitches closest to the working thread and pass your needle from right to left under the next stitch. Then pull the thread snug.

back

2 Continuing away from the end of the embroidery, take the needle under the next stitch, again with the needle passing from right to left. Pull the thread snug. You're wrapping the working thread around the embroidery stitches.

3 Repeat step 2 at least four times to secure the thread. If desired, you can reinforce and neaten the stitching by wrapping in the other direction back to where you began. Snip off the thread near the wrapping.

back

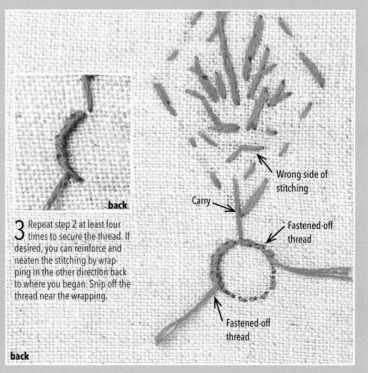

Wrong side of stitching

Carry

Fastened-off thread

Fastened-off thread

back

BASIC STITCHES

There exist hundreds of embroidery stitches. This book describes just the ones most popular with today's stitchers. Go ahead and experiment with different stitch lengths, but try to keep them uniform.

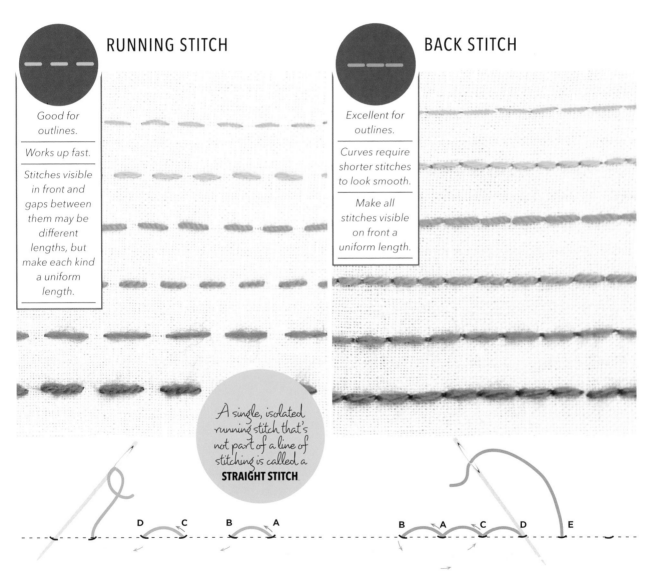

RUNNING STITCH

Good for outlines.

Works up fast.

Stitches visible in front and gaps between them may be different lengths, but make each kind a uniform length.

BACK STITCH

Excellent for outlines.

Curves require shorter stitches to look smooth.

Make all stitches visible on front a uniform length.

A single, isolated running stitch that's not part of a line of stitching is called a **STRAIGHT STITCH**.

Bring the needle up through the fabric at **(A)**, then go down at **(B)**, pulling the thread taut. Bring the needle back up at **(C)** and then go back down at **(D)**. Continue in this fashion.

Bring your needle up through the fabric at **(A)**, then go down at **(B)**. Come back up at **(C)**, pull the thread taut, then go back down at **(A)**. Bring the needle up at **(D)**, pull the thread taut, then go down at **(C)**. Come up at **(E)**, pull taut, then down at **(D)**. Continue in this pattern.

LEGEND

The fibers are shown larger than actual size.

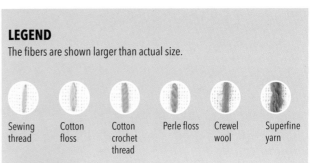

| Sewing thread | Cotton floss | Cotton crochet thread | Perle floss | Crewel wool | Superfine yarn |

SPLIT STITCH

Good for outlines, somewhat good for fills when worked with thick thread.

Use doubled thread or even numbers of strands.

Best worked with longer stitches.

CHAIN STITCH

Creates thick outlines.

Excellent for fills, especially in parallel rows.

Best worked with longer stitches. Keep thread slightly loose so curves stay rounded.

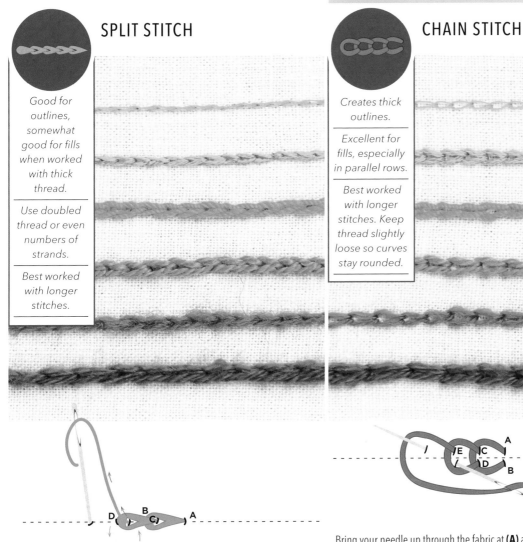

Bring your needle up through the fabric at **(A)** then go down at **(B)**. Bring it back up at **(C)**, which is halfway between **(A)** and **(B)**. At **(C)**, make sure the needle pierces between the threads, and pull the thread taut. Go back down at **(D)**. Continue in this manner.

Bring your needle up through the fabric at **(A)** and go back down at **(B)**, leaving a large loop rather than pulling the thread taut. Bring the needle back up at **(C)**, go through the loop, and pull the thread loosely to allow it to form a curve. Go back down at **(D)**, leaving a large loop instead of pulling the thread taut. Bring the needle back up at **(E)**, go through the loop, and pull the thread, but only loosely.

STEM STITCH

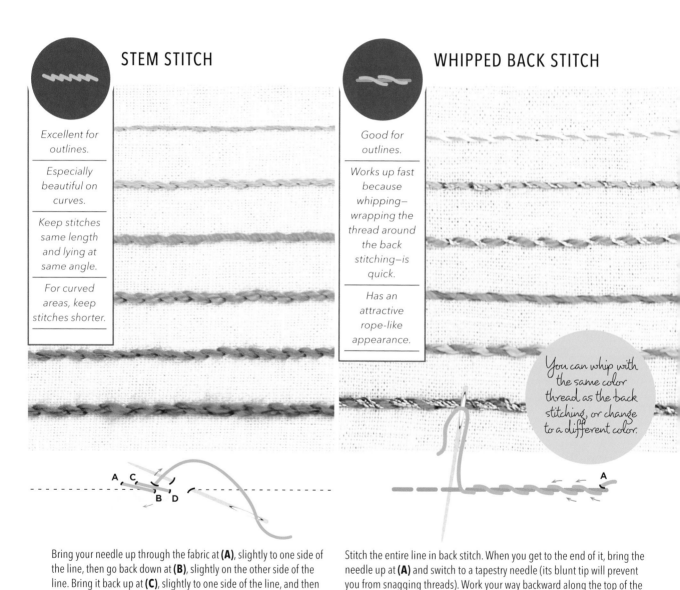

Excellent for outlines.

Especially beautiful on curves.

Keep stitches same length and lying at same angle.

For curved areas, keep stitches shorter.

WHIPPED BACK STITCH

Good for outlines.

Works up fast because whipping— wrapping the thread around the back stitching—is quick.

Has an attractive rope-like appearance.

You can whip with the same color thread as the back stitching, or change to a different color.

Bring your needle up through the fabric at **(A)**, slightly to one side of the line, then go back down at **(B)**, slightly on the other side of the line. Bring it back up at **(C)**, slightly to one side of the line, and then go back down at **(D)**, slightly on the other side of the line. Continue in this fashion.

Stitch the entire line in back stitch. When you get to the end of it, bring the needle up at **(A)** and switch to a tapestry needle (its blunt tip will prevent you from snagging threads). Work your way backward along the top of the back stitching as follows: Going from top to bottom, pass the needle under the first back stitch without going through the fabric. Going from top to bottom, pass the needle under the next stitch without going through the fabric; repeat to wrap the back stitch all the way to the end.

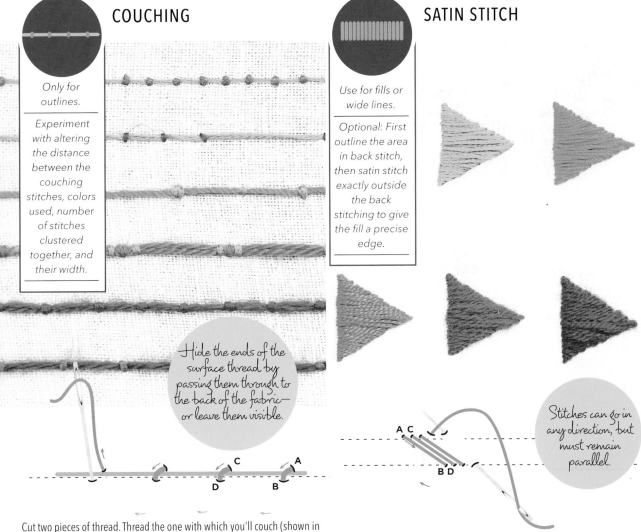

COUCHING

Only for outlines.

Experiment with altering the distance between the couching stitches, colors used, number of stitches clustered together, and their width.

Hide the ends of the surface thread by passing them through to the back of the fabric— or leave them visible.

SATIN STITCH

Use for fills or wide lines.

Optional: First outline the area in back stitch, then satin stitch exactly outside the back stitching to give the fill a precise edge.

Stitches can go in any direction, but must remain parallel.

Cut two pieces of thread. Thread the one with which you'll couch (shown in pink) on the needle. The other will simply lie on the surface of the fabric (shown in orange); as you work, arrange it to follow the line. Bring your needle up through the fabric at **(A)**, then down at **(B)**. Bring it up at **(C)**, then down at **(D)**. Continue in this manner.

Bring the needle up through the fabric at **(A)** then go down at **(B)**. Bring it back up at **(C)** and then go down at **(D)**. Continue in this manner.

SEED STITCH

Only for fills.

Length and orientation of stitches may vary.

Thread color may vary in a single area.

Bring your needle up through the fabric at **(A)** then go back down at **(B)**. Bring it back up at **(C)** and then go back down at **(D)**. Bring it back up at **(E)** and down at **(F)**. Continue in this fashion, meandering around as desired within the boundary of the area to fill.

FRENCH KNOT

Use for fills, for lines, or as a stand-alone stitch.

Wrapping the needle additional times in step 1 makes knot larger.

1

Bring the needle up through the fabric. Wrap the thread twice around the needle.

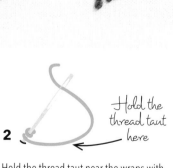

2 Hold the thread taut here

Hold the thread taut near the wraps with your thumb and index, and slowly go back down exactly where you originally came up. As the thread is ready to knot up on the fabric, let go with your fingers and gently pull the thread through. Excessive tightening ruins the knot.

HERRINGBONE STITCH

Only for lines.

Make stitch lengths and angles uniform.

Optional: After completing row, add straight stitches

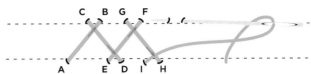

Bring the needle up through the fabric at **(A)** and down at **(B)**. Bring it back up at **(C)** and down at **(D)**. To start the next stitch, bring the needle back up at **(E)** and down at **(F)**. Come back up at (G) and down at **(H)**. Continue in this manner.

FLY STITCH

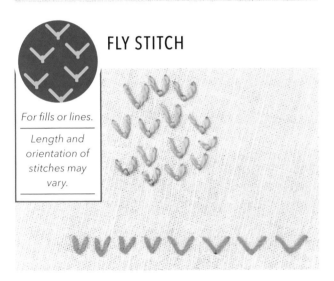

For fills or lines.

Length and orientation of stitches may vary.

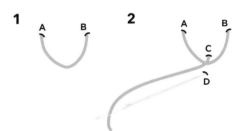

1 Bring the needle up through the fabric at **(A)**, then go down at **(B)**. Leave a large, loose loop of thread rather than pulling it tight.

2 Bring the needle up at **(C)**, pass over the loop, go down at **(D)**, and pull the thread tight to form a "V."

LAZY DAISY

A stand-alone stitch.

Length of petals may vary, but they should all be identical on a single flower.

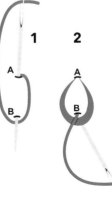

1 Bring the needle up through the fabric at **(A)**, and go back down at **(A)**, leaving a large, loose loop of thread instead of pulling it tight. Bring the needle up at **(B)**.

2 Go back down at **(B)**, making sure to pass over the loop, and pull the thread loosely to allow it to form a curve. This is called a link stitch. Stitch five more link stitches in a ring, all starting at the center.

MAKING PATCHES

Although originally intended to cover up holes, patches are again having a fashion moment. Using a thick fabric allows patches to stand away from the surface of whatever object you attach them to, so they're frequently made out of felt—often two stacked layers of it.

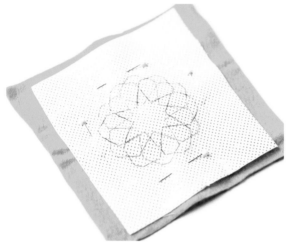

1 TRANSFER THE MOTIF
Use the transfer method of your choice. (For this wool felt, the motif was transferred onto tear-away stabilizer which was then pinned to the fabric.) Place the fabric in the hoop.

2 EMBROIDER
Stitch the motif, then take the fabric out of the hoop. (In this case, before removing the fabric from the hoop, the stabilizer was gently torn away.)

3 CUT THE SHAPE
Lightly trace the desired outline on the front of the fabric, then use sharp fabric shears to cut immediately inside that line.

4 BLANKET STITCH THE EDGE
Thread the needle with a piece of thread that's at least four times the circumference of the patch. Starting anywhere, blanket stitch all around the exterior.

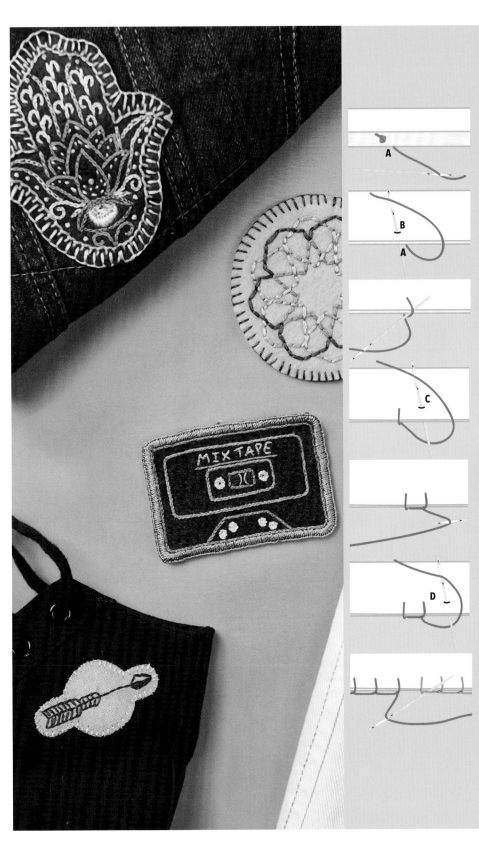

HOW TO BLANKET STITCH

1 Knot the floss. To hide the knot between the layers, pass your needle between them and go down through just the bottom piece of fabric at **A**, which is ¼ inch (6mm) from the edge.

2 Take the needle down through both layers at **B**, which is on the top layer and exactly over **A**. Pull the thread tight.

3 Working from left to right, pass the needle through the loop, at the edge. Pull the thread tight. It is now anchored.

4 Now you begin stitching. Take the needle down through both layers at **C**, making sure the needle passes over the working thread.

5 As you pull the thread tight, make sure it lies neatly against the edge of the layers of fabric.

6 Take the needle down through both layers at **D**, making sure the needle passes over the working thread. As you pull the thread tight, make sure it lies neatly against the edge of the layers of fabric. Repeat this step to work your way around the edge of the patch.

7 When you get back around to the beginning, connect the last stitch to the first (shown in gray) by passing under and through the first edge loop. Pull the thread tight, and catch the same loop a second time while knotting. To hide the end of the thread, poke the needle through the layers at the edge and exit anywhere in the middle of the patch, then trim the thread right at the surface.

CABOCHONS AND BEZELS
Make small embroidery more dimensional by mounting it on a cabochon—a small glass dome—held by a metal setting called a bezel. Look for circular 25mm cabs, as well as ovals measuring 30 x 40mm.

BAMBOO HOOP
These inexpensive hoops only grip fabric loosely, making them better suited for displaying embroidery.

3D-PRINTED HOOP
With a decorative surface texture and scalloped edges, 3D-printed frames come in a rainbow of colors.

SMALL WOODEN HOOPS
At less than 2 inches (5cm) in diameter, laser-cut wooden hoops are light enough to use as pendants.

VINTAGE METAL HOOP
The different types of closures make antique hoops visually intriguing as mechanisms for display.

VINTAGE METAL HOOPS
If they have an aged patina, it only makes them more attractive.

DISPLAYING FINISHED WORK

As you'll see when you flip through the pages of this book, many options exist for displaying embroidery. The most obvious method for showing off your work is to stretch the fabric in a different hoop than the one you use to stitch.

HOOPS

Look for hoops both vintage and new. Craft stores sell inexpensive wooden or bamboo hoops for displaying embroidery. You'll also find flexi hoops, which are made of plastic with a wood grain finish. An ornate metal handle lets you hang them on a nail.

Recent additions to the hoop options on the market include really little laser-cut wooden hoops and 3D-printed plastic frames; you're more likely to find these online than in brick and mortar stores.

CABOCHONS & BEZELS

Transform tiny embroidery into jewelry by mounting it on a glass cabochon held in a bezel. To do this, trim the fabric so it wraps partway around the flat back of the cabochon. Stitch the fabric edges to each other on the back, making sure to leave some of the glass uncovered. Then use a permanent craft adhesive such as E6000 to bond the glass cabochon—not the fabric—to the metal bezel. Allow to dry. Finally, connect the bezel with jump rings to whatever you desire—some chain, for example, or other bezels.

MOUNTING IN A HOOP

You can follow this process through step 3 and call the piece ready to hang, but the frayed edge of the fabric may bother you. If so, take the optional step of covering it up with felt.

1 Center the display hoop on the back of the stitched fabric. Measure the hoop. Double that number, then subtract 1 inch (2.5 cm). Sketch a circle of that size around the hoop.

2 Cut out the circle. Mount the fabric in the hoop with the motif face up. With the fabric face down and using thread longer than the circumference, begin basting around the edge, ½ inch (1.3cm) from it.

3 Finish basting around, then knot together both ends of the thread to tightly cinch the fabric. Double knot to hold it permanently. Tuck the knot and thread inside to hide them.

OPTIONAL
If desired, camouflage the frayed edge of the fabric by cutting a felt circle slightly larger than the opening and attach it with fabric glue.

To display, prop against any vertical surface, or stitch on a ribbon loop or attach a safety pin to hang it on a nail.

MOUNTING FABRIC ON A STRETCHER

Art supply stores sell premade stretchers in standard sizes, and can also build them in custom dimensions and depths.

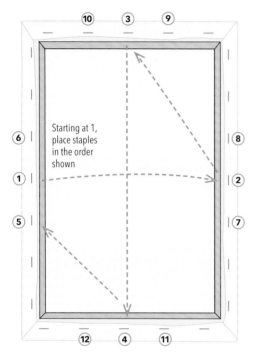

Starting at 1, place staples in the order shown

THEN FOLD THE CORNERS

This creates a neat fold along the sides of the top and bottom edges. Work on one corner at a time–it doesn't matter which.

1 Pull the fabric taut along either one of the sides–not the top or bottom– then place a staple.

2 Pull the fabric across the corner at an angle roughly 30° from the top of the stretcher. This will create a fold. Don't place a staple yet. Instead, hold the fabric in place with one hand on the inside of the corner.

FIRST STAPLE THE SIDES

Iron out the wrinkles in the embroidery. Arrange the fabric as desired on the front of the stretcher. Holding it in place, flip the stretcher to work on the back. Smooth out the fabric. Using a heavy-duty staple gun with the appropriate staples, place the first staple in the middle of one long side of the stretcher–it doesn't matter which. Pull firmly on the fabric on the stretcher across from staple 1, but not so much that you distort the fabric. Place the second staple.

Place the third staple in the middle of either one of the short sides. Pull the fabric on the stretcher across from staple 3 taut, without distorting the fabric. Check the front to make sure it doesn't look warped, then place staple 4.

Working on alternate sides, place staples on either side of the existing staples until most of the length of the sides is stapled. Leave roughly 2 inches (5cm) unstapled at the corners so you can make neat folds. Trim off any fabric extending past the stretcher.

3 With the other hand, pull the fabric down over the top of the stretcher, using your fingers to gently fold it in exactly along the corner of the stretcher.

4 Place a staple at the side to hold the fold. Then place staples between the corner and the side staples, smoothing and stretching the fabric flat as needed. Cut any fabric that extends past the stretcher at this corner. Repeat all steps on the remaining corners.

FABRIC APPLIQUÉ

To attach a small piece of shaped fabric–called an appliqué–to the foundation fabric, use paper-backed fusible web.

! Shapes will be reversed by this process, so always start with a motif that's a mirror image of the desired final appliqué.

IDENTIFYING THE SIDES OF PAPER-BACKED FUSIBLE WEB

The rough side has heat-actived glue; the smooth face is paper that peels off. Once you remove the paper, it exposes more heat-activated glue.

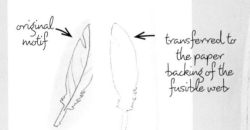

original motif

transferred to the paper backing of the fusible web

1 Tape the original motif–it should be a reverse image of the final desired image–to a window. Place the fusible web on it with the paper backing facing you. Then trace the motif onto the paper backing. Remove from window, and untape and discard the original motif.

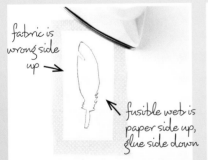

fabric is wrong side up

fusible web is paper side up, glue side down

2 Turn on the iron, with steam off. Place the fabric face down on the ironing board. Leaving the paper backing on, place the glue side of the fusible web against the fabric. Press briefly with the iron until the fusible web adheres to the fabric.

3 Cut out the motif. Peel off the paper backing, exposing the glue. Place the appliqué right side up (and therefore glue side down) on the right side of the foundation fabric. Press briefly until it fuses to the fabric.

4 Embroider as desired.

COMMUNICATION

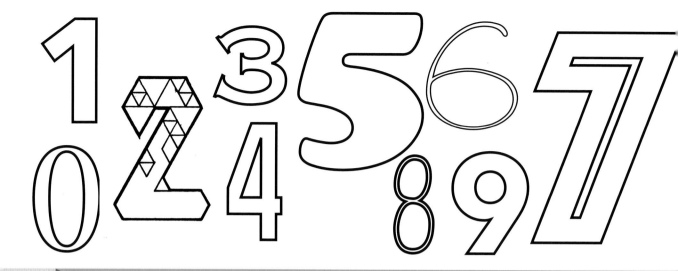

NUMBERS

Embroider numbers to memorialize special dates, addresses, birthdays, and anniversaries. The more unusual the font, the more striking the finished stitching, so look for unique lettering styles.

▼ COMBINE PAINT & FLOSS

After very lightly drawing the motif on watercolor paper in 4H pencil–so it doesn't smudge later–apply a light wash of watercolor paint. No problem if it dribbles. Create a heavy **back-stitched** outline with six strands of floss; use only two for the geometric interior sections.

▲ PAD THE STITCHING

To make the edge look super crisp and raise the numbers off the surface of the fabric, pad the design before you stitch. To do so, cut out numbers from heavy cardstock. Stretch the fabric in a hoop, and use white craft glue to adhere the numbers to the cloth. After the glue has dried, **satin stitch** over the cardstock.

USE A DEEP FRAME
A large piece 23 x 17 inches (58.5 x 43cm) looks more impactful raised away from the wall on a custom stretcher 2 ½ inches (6 mm) deep. The numbers stitch up faster in yarn. Outline them in a mix of **running stitch** and **whipped back stitch**.

▲ ADD TEXTURE
A banner holds a child's name in fanciful letters worked in **satin stitch** and **back stitch**.

▼ MODIFY A MOTTO
A font that looks engraved is the perfect choice for a Latin phrase rewritten to encourage the reader to seize the night. It's made in **satin stitch**.

COMMUNICATION

➤ WORDS

You can do so much with words: Place a friend's name on a T-shirt, stitch in a foreign language, embroider cheeky adjectives on accessories, proclaim your motto in a framed canvas or on a garment ...

◀ DECORATE A HEM
Declare your true nature by emblazoning the word "trouble" along the bottom of a skirt. The can't-miss letters stand out in a bold **satin stitch** embroidered in perle cotton.

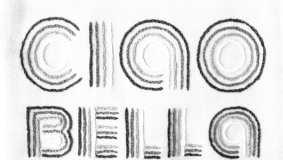

STITCH PARALLEL LINES ▶
Ciao, bella–that's Italian for "hello, gorgeous." The four parallel lines of **split stitching** in perle cotton range from a navy blue to bluish gray, emphasizing the Art Deco font style.

SPIFF UP A
SIDE SEAM

Select a fun word to stitch and place it in an unexpected spot–along the side seam of a T-shirt. Apply it with cotton crochet thread, outlining it in **split stitch** and filling it with a playful dotting of widely spaced **French knots**.

BLEND TWO SHADES

Some of these **French knots** are stitched in a mustard color, others are blue, but look closely and you'll see that at least a third of them are made in a combination of mustard and blue. This helps meld two very different hues.

WORDS

It's fun to embroider unexpected words or concepts. Embroidery may seem old-fashioned to some, so make your words serve as a witty contrast. You might consider slang, snarky sayings, and even profanity.

◄ ADD MEANING

A word like "cool," with multiple definitions, adds a layer of substance to an old family photo. Was the day cool in temperature? Is this a lady who always keeps her composure? Was she on a trip to someplace hip? Choose a bold font and run it as large as possible. In this case, the word is outlined in **split stitch** in the photo's defining color: white.

▲ OUTLINE IN KNOTS

"Fizz" describes the effervescent whisper of bubbles. Stitched on a photo of a frozen waterfall, it reflects that icebound liquid–its bubbles trapped in time, like the text trapped on the page with droplet-like **French knots**.

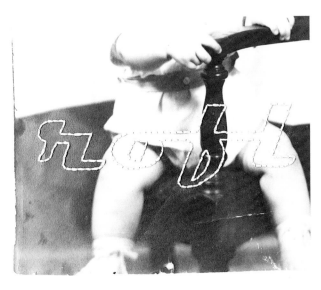

▲ JUXTAPOSE ERAS

Back stitch an Internet acronym like "ROFL" onto a photo dating back to the 1930s to create a strange sort of time warp. Here, the infant's cropped head only adds to the oddness of the effect.

▲ CHOOSE AN OLD FONT

A delicate Art Nouveau font works up nicely in **chain stitch**. The font looks a little spooky, reinforcing the supernatural meaning behind the word, and the open stitch looks good with the tall, skinny letters.

▲ OUTLINE HEAVILY

A bold outline in six strands of **split stitch** is a good choice for a word as heavily charged as "satyr." The rough, hairy surface of the felt subtly echoes the animality of a satyr–a lustful, drunken woodland god from Greek mythology. The neon shade of floss helps it stand out against the fuzzy fabric.

STITCH ON PAPER

Take your embroidery in an unusual direction by stitching on paper. Follow these tips for success.

- Always reinforce the paper by attaching a piece of fusible stabilizer to the entire back of the sheet before stitching.

- Stiffer paper is better than limp. Stabilizer comes in various weights, so for limper paper, select thicker stabilizer.

- To transfer the motif, either pierce the lines of the design with a push pin or needle, draw it on the back of the paper—remember to reverse it–or draw it on the front and stitch with a thick enough thread to completely cover it.

- The fiber must be bigger around than the needle, or the holes made by the needle will show.

- Knot the ends of your floss or fiber. Don't make waste knots or fasten off.

- Place the work flat on the table to support it as you slowly and gently pull the thread through.

- Replace the floss often. When it rubs against paper, it frays faster than it does against fabric.

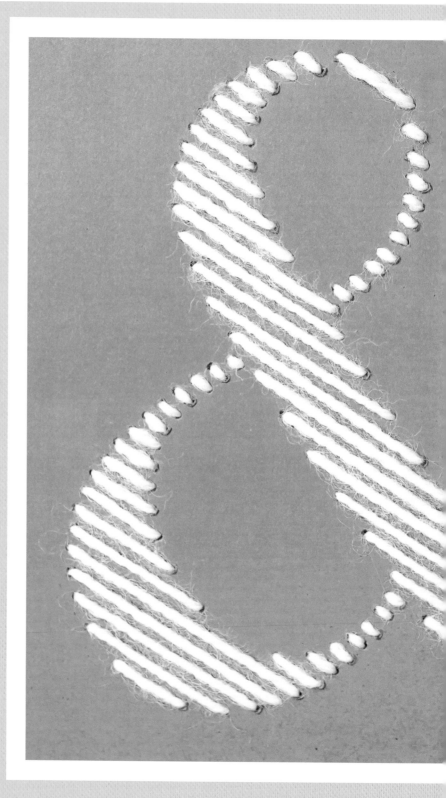

EMBROIDER AN AMPERSAND

Try out this project as a primer for embroidering on paper.
The finer your graph paper, the closer together the
diagonal strips of yarn. Don't like ampersands? Choose
any strong, graphic shape as the motif.

What you'll need

Graph paper
Sheet of paper containing
  the motif
Pen or pencil
Fusible interfacing

Iron and ironing board
Paper to embroider on
Push pin
Small tapestry needle
Yarn

1 You'll use the window transfer method in this step. Tape the graph paper to
the window with the lines at an angle rather than on a horizontal or vertical
axis. Tape the motif over it. Trace over the graph lines only where they intersect
with the motif.

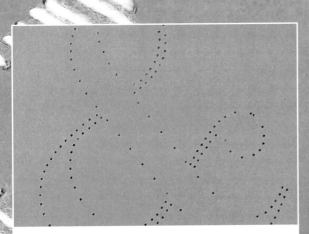

2 Turn on the iron with the steam off and fuse the interfacing to the back of
the paper on which you'll embroider. Place the paper face up on a soft
but firm surface, such as an ironing board. Put the motif face up on it.
Holding the motif in place, use a push pin to pierce holes at each
intersection of the motif and the graph lines.

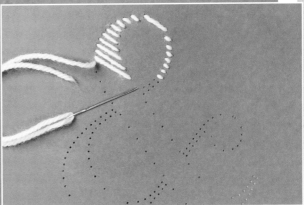

3 Thread the tapestry needle with yarn. Knot the end of the yarn and stitch the
diagonal lines. You may find it handy to refer to the original motif to make
sure to connect the correct dots.

AMPERSANDS

With their strong graphic sensibility, ampersands have become icons in typography. They originated as a logogram for the Latin word "et," which means "and," and they come in many different font styles.

▼ CREATE A COLOR GRADIENT

Use a band of **satin stitch** ¼ inch (6 mm) wide to create a bold outline on a toss pillow for your couch. The stitching gradually blends from light to dark to create a shaded effect called ombré.

▲ CROP THE MOTIF

Any symbol with an unmistakable, distinct shape can have part of its edges cut off and still remain recognizable. The ampersand on this wall canvas is filled with stripes of **chain stitch**. After being stitched, it was mounted onto a frame that's slightly smaller than the motif.

FILL WITH KNOTS

A blanket of **French knots** fills the motif, which is stitched on a coin purse. At this density, the knots literally stand off the surface to create an additional layer of texture on the fabric.

The color of the lining influenced the choice of thread colors.

▼ STITCH ON PAPER

Find an old book in a foreign language. Tear out a page and embroider a letter in a dimensional font on it. Frame it. Boom—you've got a really cool piece of art for your wall.

▼ BOOST THE FONT

The original font chosen for this **satin-stitched** pouch was quite plain. Adding curlicues and elongating the serifs made it more elaborate and fun to look at.

MONOGRAMS

Monogramming is the ultimate personalization. Perfect canvases for it include pj's, coasters, fabric purses and totes, and shirt pockets, plackets, and cuffs. If it's not monogrammed, does it even really belong to you?

▲ PERSONALIZE A BROOCH

A small oval brooch blank leaves just enough space for a single letter. Created in black **satin stitch**, it stands out boldly from the linen behind it. A larger blank allows for more letters.

▲ OUTLINE IT WIDE

Monogram a keepsake ornament with a single letter outlined in **satin stitch**. Instead of filling it with another shade of satin stitch, place just a few evenly placed horizontal bars of satin stitch for a striped effect.

SHADOW WORK
Starbursts of **straight stitch** and **French knots** surround letter shapes on a canvas banner. Thick and glossy, perle cotton is a good choice for this technique because the heavy thread contrasts with the negative space. Stitch the initials of someone's name—or of an educational institution to show your school spirit.

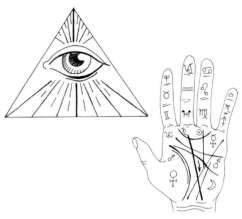

MYSTIC SYMBOLS

If you're a seeker of higher consciousness or hidden truths, imagery associated with your path may be the perfect motif. As you slowly embroider, you can meditate on your spiritual journey.

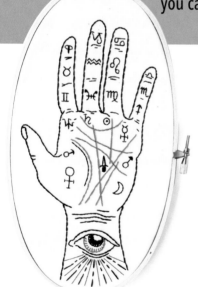

▲ COMBINE MOTIFS

Part of the all-seeing eye motif was added to the palmistry hand design. Although there's a lot going on in this embroidery, it's all tied together by the simple palette of black and red.

▼ KEEP IT SUBTLE

Reveal your conspiracy-theorizing self–or your sense of humor–by placing a small Eye of Providence, associated with the Illuminati, on a shirt cuff. The **straight stitches** at the bottom employ two strands for the longer lines and a single strand for the short ones.

LIMIT THE COLORS

Blue stitching on a deep blue felt background stays within a narrow color palette. That helps the lotus, as the focal point stitched in complementary orange, stand out from the rest of the design. This highly textural patch has embroidery in very fine **chain stitch**, **split stitch**, **blanket stitch**, and **French knots**, with the eye in **satin stitch**. Patches can be made in virtually any shape—the more unusual, the better!

Blanket stitch the edge of the patch first, then stitch it to the denim.

ASTROLOGY

Hey, man, what's your sign? From Aquarius to Capricorn, everybody's got one. Find out someone's birthday or zodiac sign and you can then personalize embroidery for them and give it as a gift.

▼ INCLUDE METALLIC THREAD

Add one strand of metallic thread to your six strands of cotton floss for a subtle shimmer. Then **back stitch** and **satin stitch** the motif. Finally, mount it in a brass ring blank with a bezel cup.

▲ DECORATE THE BACKGROUND

The motif for this brooch was **satin stitched** in gray, then further detailed with **straight stitches** in red. Red crossed stitches placed around the motif add a bit more visual interest to the fabric.

REVERSE APPLIQUÉ

This patch is as much about negative space as it is about embroidery. The motif was cut out of the center of a piece of felt, leaving behind an empty space. The remaining pieces were pinned to another piece of felt and held down with **running stitch**. A border of sequins and beads edge the patch, which is applied to a felt bag.

TATTOO FLASH

Tattoo-themed motifs are perfect for the person who doesn't want to commit to permanent ink, but also fun for tattoo addicts who can't get enough. These motifs are based on tattoo designs–known as flash–from the World War II era.

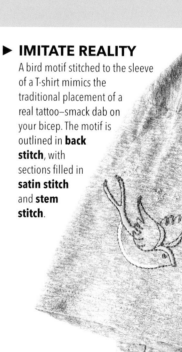

▶ IMITATE REALITY

A bird motif stitched to the sleeve of a T-shirt mimics the traditional placement of a real tattoo–smack dab on your bicep. The motif is outlined in **back stitch**, with sections filled in **satin stitch** and **stem stitch**.

▲ ENHANCE THE EDGE

While the **satin stitching** in this rose looks striking, what really helps this design pop is the doubled lines of stitching–using two strands of yellow and sea green, respectively–that bring out the single-strand **back-stitched** edges of the leaves.

GIVE BABY A TAT
Baby will look badass in a denim bandana bib emblazoned with a vintage anchor. The doubled strands used for the **back stitching** give the design a solid visual presence. Red **satin stitching** adds pops of color.

DAY OF THE DEAD

This Mexican holiday honoring the deceased has exuberant, colorful, and creepy-fun iconography that's perfect to embroider on costumes. It's celebrated, with gusto, between October 31 and November 2.

▶ MIX THREAD WEIGHTS

This skull uses two-stranded **split stitch** for the heavy outlines and a single strand for the interior details. The small **French knots** under the brow ridge have fewer strands than the large ones at the center of the eye. This variety of line widths create a lot of visual interest on the tag.

▼ STITCH NEON ON BLACK

Celebrate the Day of the Dead in a little black skirt adorned with a fitting motif. Outline in **stem stitch**, with fills in **seed stitch**, using two strands. Against the black, the seed stitches look like beads.

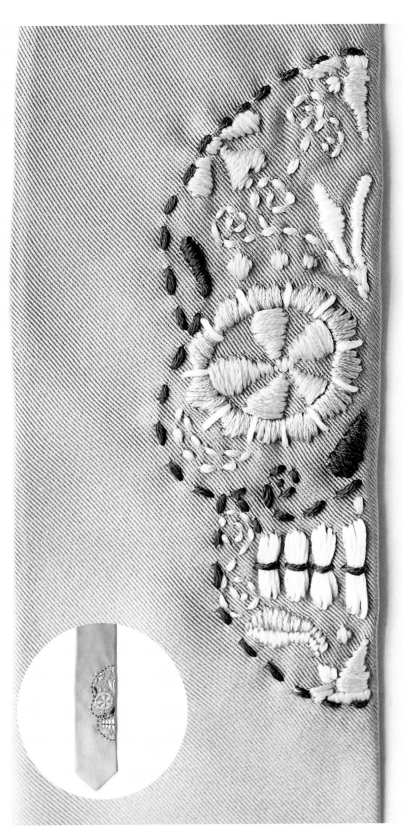

CROP OFF HALF

Cut off half the motif–it lets you embroider it larger on a tie and looks more interesting. The design is worked in **running stitch** and **satin stitch**. Note that the pearly whites consist of tall sections of **satin stitch** cinched around the middle with a horizontal **straight stitch** to look like top teeth stacked on bottom teeth.

The different lengths of satin stitch around the eye sockets resemble petals.

NATURAL WORLD

AQUATIC LIFE

Some sea creatures, like shells and seahorses, are traditional in the decorative arts. More unusual-looking animals, like the octopus, narwhal, and squid, are a recent, trendy addition to the roster of animal motifs in crafts.

▼ CREATE A BORDER

Repeat the motif as many times as needed to form a row. Here, four sand dollars bedeck the top edge of the side pocket on a canvas beach tote. Detailed in thick **chain stitch** with **French knot** details, the color shifts from navy on the left to pale blue on the right.

▲ SHRINK IT

Tiny seashells fit neatly into oval earring blanks. Worked in **back stitch** in an orangey red, they stand out against the navy background fabric.

USE BAKER'S TWINE

The thickness of baker's twine causes it to rest on the base fabric rather than lie snugly in it, so it stands in relief on the cloth. It matches the blue and white vintage-style napkins perfectly, and couldn't be a better fit for a nautical theme. Because both sides of napkins are visible, try to keep your **stem stitch** as perfect and knotless on the back as it is on the front.

WOODLAND CREATURES

Cute animals are a standard embroidery motif. However, they go through trends, so the types of critters that are popular and the ways they're represented change with time.

▲ JUST SATIN STITCH

A wee raccoon adorns a small wooden brooch. **Satin stitch** fills the entire design, giving a small image a lot of impact.

▼ FILL IT DENSELY

Arrange the **stem stitching** on Mr. Hedgehog in undulating rows for the spines–placing them so close they almost look like satin stitch–and in columns for his body. The spines include a mix of analogous pinks and reds. **Satin stitch** his ear, cheek, and eye.

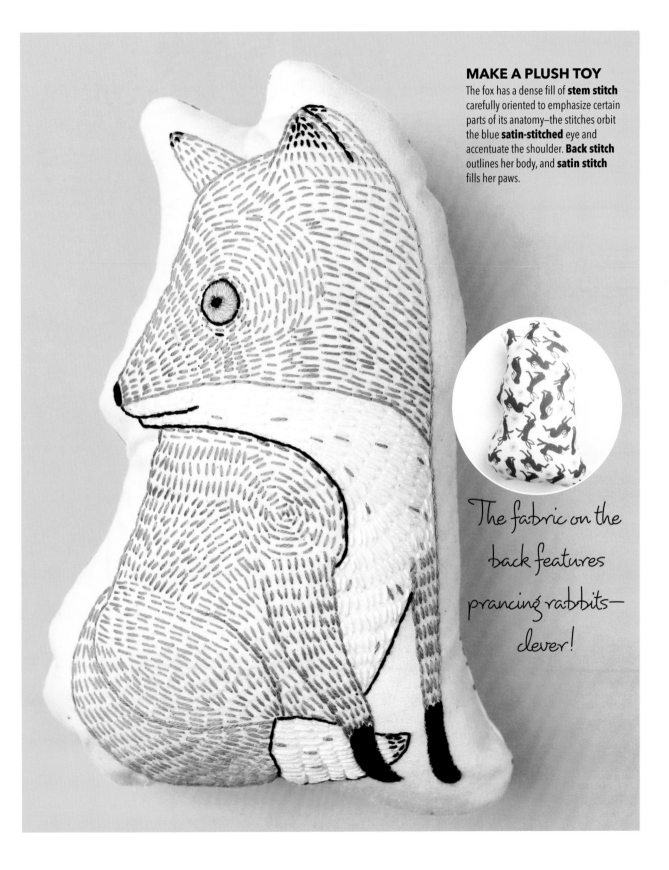

MAKE A PLUSH TOY

The fox has a dense fill of **stem stitch** carefully oriented to emphasize certain parts of its anatomy–the stitches orbit the blue **satin-stitched** eye and accentuate the shoulder. **Back stitch** outlines her body, and **satin stitch** fills her paws.

The fabric on the back features prancing rabbits— clever!

DEER

Antlers are associated with the outdoorsy and rustic, while does give off a gentle vibe. Both are tied to the hipster aesthetic and the recent popularity of faux taxidermy. Combine them with geometry for still more cool.

▲ STAY MONOCHROMATIC

You can never go wrong with black–it holds so much impact! Work the outlines of the antlers with a couple strands of **split stitch**, to look heavier. The interior details look delicate in a single strand of **back stitch**.

▼ FILL IT UP

After outlining it in **back stitch**, fill the entire design with **satin stitch** in black. Center it on the back of a denim shirt, right below the yoke, to rack up fashion points.

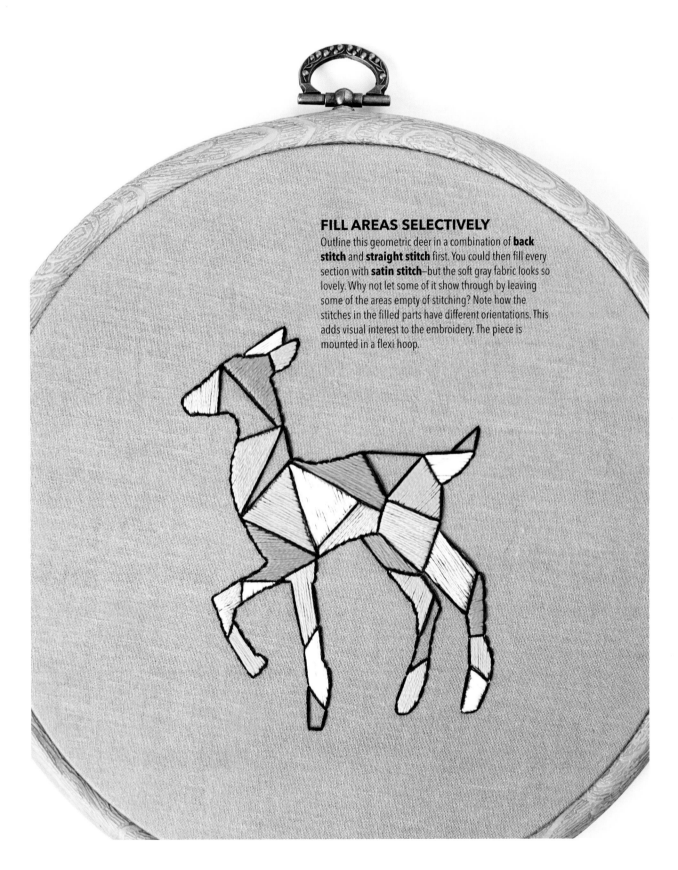

FILL AREAS SELECTIVELY

Outline this geometric deer in a combination of **back stitch** and **straight stitch** first. You could then fill every section with **satin stitch**–but the soft gray fabric looks so lovely. Why not let some of it show through by leaving some of the areas empty of stitching? Note how the stitches in the filled parts have different orientations. This adds visual interest to the embroidery. The piece is mounted in a flexi hoop.

INSECTS

With their gossamer wings and stick-like bodies, dragonflies are dramatic and striking. Butterflies and moths look like living gems. And then there are the insects we find "cute," like bees and lady bugs.

▼ USE METALLIC FLOSSES

To outline the wings in **whipped back stitch**, take a first pass in **back stitch** using cotton floss, then **whip** over it with metallic floss. This achieves an effect like twisted rope. To replicate the shimmer of real dragonfly wings, the fill inside the wings blends densely woven Diamant and Light Effects threads.

▲ FILL WITH CURLICUES

The outline on this felt ornament stands out strongly because it's stitched with six strands of floss in **chain stitch**, but it doesn't overpower the eye-catching glint of **back-stitched** metallic thread swirls.

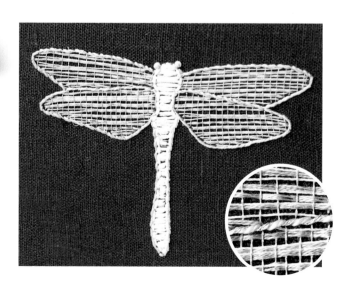

USE THICK THREAD

Size 5 perle floss—which is the heavier weight of perle—prevents the dragonflies embroidered down the side seam of a pair of jeans from getting lost on the dark fabric. Outlined in **back stitch**, they're filled with **straight stitches**. A few clusters of crossed **straight stitches** placed here and there help tie the insect motifs together.

▶ FEATHERS

In various cultures, feathers symbolize freedom, travel, truth, wisdom, power, courage, and bravery. Some people view them as communications from the spirit world. Besides, they're graceful and pretty!

▼ MIX IT UP

The three identical **back-stitched** motifs on this dish towel all look very different. That's because two of them consist of appliqués mixed with embroidery, one is a mirror image of the others, and two use two shades of thread, while the other is monochromatic.

▲ GET COLORFUL

Stripes of **back stitch** in different hues take a feather that would have been pretty in just one shade to a whole other level. It's stitched on muslin and framed in an antique metal embroidery hoop with a spring closure.

A simple outline doesn't have to stick to a single shade.

GO TWO-TONE

Two similar colors–dark coral and light peachy orange–outline the motif on this **split-stitched** felt book cover, in a ratio of roughly one to two. Those proportions are more visually interesting than if the colors had been used in equal parts.

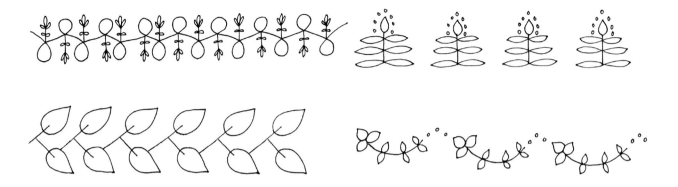

▶ PLANT BORDERS

Plant borders lend a pretty, feminine touch to whatever object they grace. Keep in mind that you can run them along the edge of your foundation fabric, down the center of it, or elsewhere. There's no single correct placement.

▶ MAKE A BOOKMARK

This bookmark, in gray cotton, combines **back-stitched** stems, **stem-stitched** outlines, and leaves filled with **seed stitch**. The orange felt backing is held on with **blanket stitch**.

▼ EMBELLISH A DEEP CUFF

Give your jeans a cuff of 3½ inches (9cm) or more and embroider it near the top. It's even better if the edge of the fabric is frayed because it adds still more texture. This entire design was completed in **chain stitch**.

STITCH WHITE ON WHITE

Whitework refers to any type of embroidery where the thread color is the same shade as the foundation fabric. Traditionally, the technique would have combined white thread on a white linen ground, but nowadays any monochromatic palette in any hue gets this name. The motif on this shirt placket has been **back stitched**.

▶ LEAVES

With leaves, you have so many shape options, from the delicate paired leaflets of the acacia or locust to pretty heart-shaped ivy and on to the large and burly oak. How will you ever decide which to stitch?

▼ LEAVE EDGES RAW

Cutouts of leaves are loosely attached to a table runner along the stem and veins only, rather than along the exterior–in other words, they're not held on with fusible interfacing. The edges, left raw, or unfinished, give a romantically shabby suggestion of fallen leaves. This design uses a mix of **running**, **stem**, **chain**, and **back stitch**.

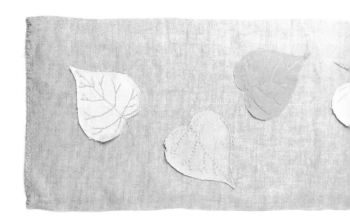

▲ REVERSE THE IMAGE

Instead of stitching the lines of the motif, **satin stitch** all around them. The stem line of the leaf on this ornament is stitched, however–using **chain stitch**, which is wide, so that it doesn't disappear into the fuzzy felt.

STITCH YARN ON YARN

Variegated crewel yarn shows up well on warm woolen mittens. The stem is sewn, appropriately enough, in **stem stitch**, while the yarn for the leaves is loosely held down with **couching**.

SHADOW WORK

Stitching around a motif, instead of along its outline or inside it, creates an interesting effect with negative space. You can use any color of foundation fabric and thread, but combining dark cloth and white thread packs a highly dramatic punch.

What you'll need

Transfer materials
Motif
Fabric
Embroidery hoop
Needle and floss
Embroidery scissors

1 Use any method to transfer the motif onto the cloth. For this dark fabric, the motif was cut out of the paper, pinned to the cloth, and traced with a white transfer pencil. The paper was then removed in preparation for stitching.

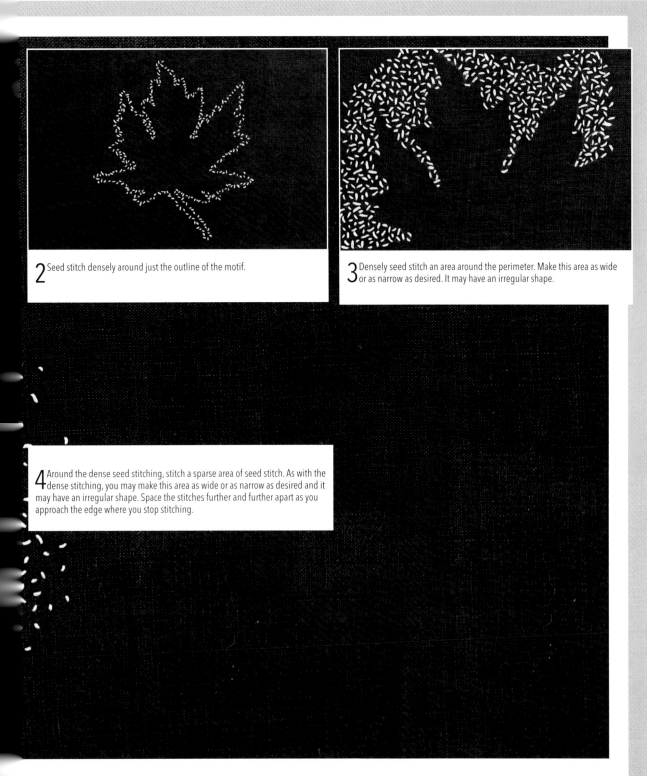

2 Seed stitch densely around just the outline of the motif.

3 Densely seed stitch an area around the perimeter. Make this area as wide or as narrow as desired. It may have an irregular shape.

4 Around the dense seed stitching, stitch a sparse area of seed stitch. As with the dense stitching, you may make this area as wide or as narrow as desired and it may have an irregular shape. Space the stitches further and further apart as you approach the edge where you stop stitching.

CACTUS

Cacti and succulents are the plants du jour. You see them everywhere: in magazine spreads, in restaurant and shop décor, in vintage tea cups at your friend's apartment. They're cute and very embroiderable.

▼ COLOR DISCERNINGLY

Heavy outlines and thin interior lines give this embroidery a nicely stark, graphic quality. That aspect is enhanced by the black **satin-stitched** shading and the yellow sections on the pot. The improvised yellow flowers soften the look.

▼ EMBELLISH THE POCKET

Embroidering on a breast pocket is so predictable. Instead, look for unconventional spots to stitch. A few little embroidered potted cacti look adorable lined up in a row below the pocket on a pair of jeans.

ADD COLOR TO WHITEWORK

A whitework cactus, outlined in **chain stitch**, has interior lines worked in **running stitch** to create a pronounced variation in line weight. The flowers, in **straight stitch**, add splashes of color.

FLOWERS

Flowers are a traditional embroidery motif. They run the gamut from stylized to folkloric to botanically accurate. You can stitch them in realistic colors … or let your imagination run riot.

▲ MAKE BUTTONS

Replace the buttons on your winter wool coat with embroidered buttons–instant facelift! Buy a craft cover button kit in the same size as the originals, stitch your own fabric, then assemble the buttons. With such a small surface area, it's quick and easy.

▼ PLAY WITH TEXTURES

White embroidery looks elegant and serene on any solid fabric. This folklore-inspired floral design looks quite textural with a mix of **lazy daisy**, **French knots**, **chain stitch**, and **stem stitch**.

CROP MOTIFS

Stitching through the three layers of outer pocket, watch pocket, and pocket lining would be too challenging, so part of the motif is cropped out. Keeping the pocket operational would only complicate the embroidery work—just stitch it shut.

KEEP PALETTES SIMPLE

The flowers embroidered in **running stitch**, **back stitch**, and **French knots** along the other side seam of these jeans look pretty and understated because they're in only three pale hues—and one of them is in a blue close to the color of the denim.

SEED HEADS

Dried seed heads look delicate, which makes them an ideal motif for dainty embroidery. They include dandelions, Queen Anne's lace, thistle, poppies, silver pennies, allium, cone flowers, and more.

► WOOL ON WOOL

A trio of flower motifs looks chic **chain stitched** in crewel yarn near the side seam of a straight wool skirt. Even the seeds are single chain stitches.

▼ REPEAT AND RESIZE

Duplicate the same motif in different sizes so as to blanket a rectangle of felt, using **French knots** and **back stitch**. Then sew the felt into a tube that fits snugly around a giant glass vase. The resulting decorative vase cover will hide the stems of flowers displayed inside the container.

Golden yellow stitching looks gorgeous on a gray foundation.

STITCH A SHADE

To make something like this, you'll need a kit for a fabric-covered lampshade. Embroider the design first, using **seed stitch** for the seeds and **stem stitch** for the rest of the design, then assemble the shade. Keep the back of the stitching as neat and knot-free as possible, and avoid carrying thread, because the back of the work will show through when the lamp is on and light shines through the shade.

WEATHER

Because it often affects our moods, the weather can represent an emotional state. Images of rainclouds seem melancholy, lightning bolts scream of energy, and sunrays radiate cheer.

▲ REPEAT THE MOTIF

Five motifs go all around the brim of a knit cap, four in navy to match the headwear and one in a different color to add a little visual interest. Don't forget to apply stabilizer on the back before you embroider stretchy fabrics.

▼ ADD SEQUINS

Embroider this T-shirt in two very subtly different shades of yellow, using **chain stitch** and **running stitch**. Instead of embroidering the center of the sun, fill it with a spiral of flat sequins individually attached with **back stitch**.

FLIP THE MOTIF

You never have to keep the motif oriented the way you found it. Embroider on felt to make this large bib necklace. The central circle in the motif, worked in yellow **chain stitch**, has detail work sewn over it in gold metallic **back stitch**. The rest of the motif is also produced in **back stitch**.

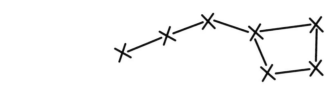

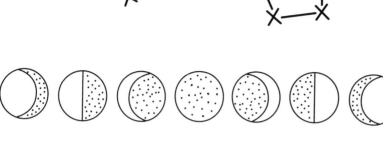
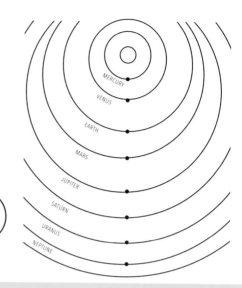

NIGHT SKY

The night sky has always fascinated humans. The stars spin mysteriously above us, and we connect them into constellations. The moon goes through its phases while exerting its pull on the tides.

▲ MAKE A PENDANT

Mount a constellation in a wee wooden frame. The stars are tiny silver "X"s. The lines between them are **straight stitches**.

▼ STITCH MOON PHASES

Because the moon has many phases, you can install motifs of the different stages–stitched in **stem stitch** and **chain stitch**–onto cabochons mounted in bezel cups, then connect them into a necklace. Each link will then feature a distinct image.

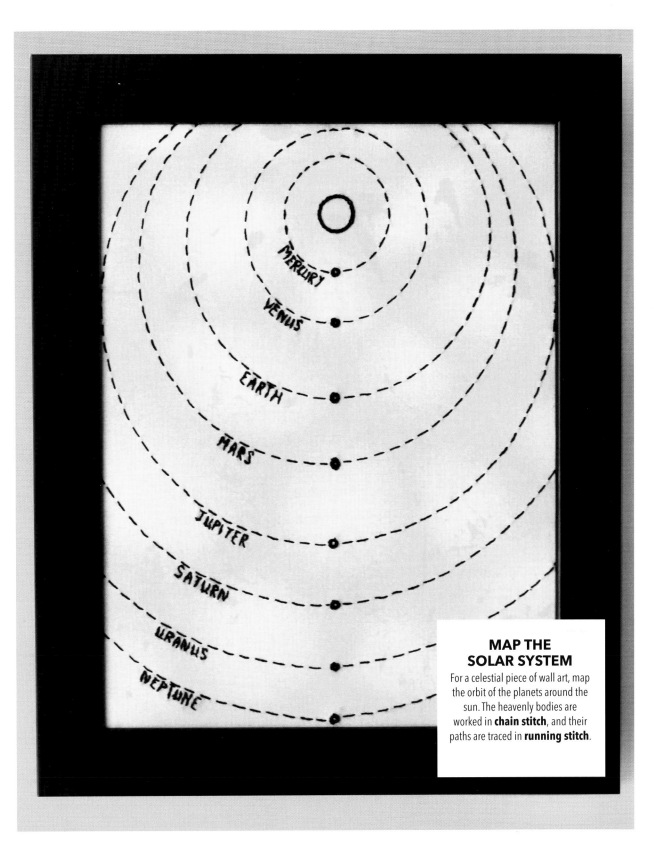

MERCURY

VENUS

EARTH

MARS

JUPITER

SATURN

URANUS

NEPTUNE

**MAP THE
SOLAR SYSTEM**

For a celestial piece of wall art, map
the orbit of the planets around the
sun. The heavenly bodies are
worked in **chain stitch**, and their
paths are traced in **running stitch**.

PEOPLE

Mysterious girls, cute kids, bearded sea captains, high-fashion ladies—people are fun to embroider because their faces and posture tell a story. Choose any angle: face-on, profile, three-quarter, back view …

▲ ADD FLOWERS

A flower with runaway petals blows past this girl's face, and a line of **running stitch** borders the edge of her sleeves.

▼ ADD THE UNEXPECTED

Fill part of the motif with another unrelated one. In this example, the girl is produced in simple black **back stitch** and **stem stitch**. A coral motif added to her forearm and upper hand is **satin stitched**.

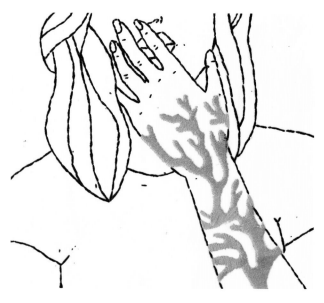

COLOR ONE
AREA

This girl is completed in a mix of **back stitch** and **stem stitch** in black. The subtle range of pastel greens in her **satin-stitched** hair is a complementary color to the pink on the two-tone tote bag upon which she's stitched.

DESIGNED WORLD

KEYS

Keys are a great motif because they represent unlocking–of love, of knowledge, of wisdom. Besides, they come in so many interesting shapes, especially European and antique keys!

▼ MAKE A HANGTAG

For an ornament hangtag to dangle off your purse or luggage, **blanket stitch** the motif on a piece of felt, then cut out the key shape close to the edge. Cut an identical key shape, again from felt, but don't embroider it. Stack the shapes with the embroidered piece on top, match the edges, and pin them together. Then stitch the edges together using sewing thread in a shade that matches the felt.

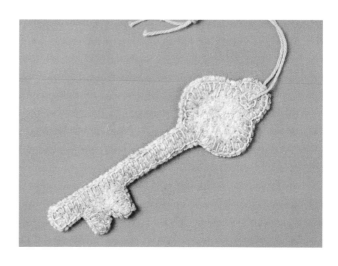

▲ STITCH ACTUAL SIZE

This antique key was produced life size using closely spaced **running stitch**. Because a cardigan stretches, before you begin you'll need to stabilize the knitting by backing the area on which you plan to embroider.

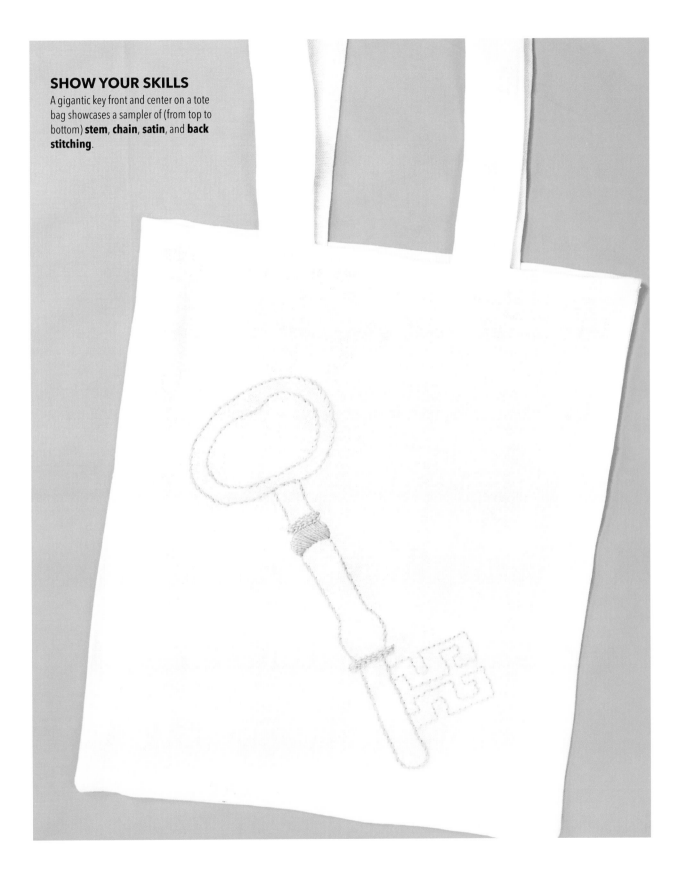

SHOW YOUR SKILLS

A gigantic key front and center on a tote bag showcases a sampler of (from top to bottom) **stem**, **chain**, **satin**, and **back stitching**.

RETRO

Old objects are always so fun: They seemed so modern in their day, but now look delightfully prehistoric! You don't have to lock into the 70s and 80s. Go with articles from any period in time.

▼ APPLIQUÉ, THEN STITCH

Just a roller skate appliqué would be fun, but adding embroidered details in **back stitch**, **blanket stitch**, and **straight stitch** takes the design up a notch.

▲ OUTLINE, THEN FILL

The Rubik's cube on this pencil case was outlined first–this was completed in **split stitch**, but you can use any stitch you like. Applying those stitches helps the edges of the **satin stitch** fill added afterward look sharp and orderly.

STITCH CLOSELY

Making closely spaced **blanket stitches** creates a dense edge that causes this patch to look almost commercially produced. The rest of the motif is stitched in **split stitch**.

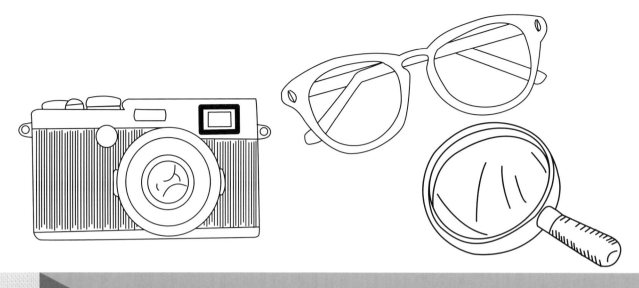

VISUAL AIDS

This category includes any number of objects that help you see better or look more closely. It includes glasses and pince-nez, smartphones and SLR cameras, and microscopes and magnifying glasses.

▲ CUSHION IT

Glasses—they're nerdy, bookish, and super-cool! Show off your geek chic in a prime location: couch cushions are a perfect canvas. **Stem stitch** is great for all those curves.

▼ ADD A PHRASE

A magnifying glass conjures up any number of short expressions about vision or seeing. The embroidery on this beach tote is all in **back stitch**. The thread color coordinates with the gray of the bag.

FRAME IT

A tiny retro camera in **back stitch** and
satin stitch takes no time to whip
together. Mount it in a small hoop–this
one measures only 2 inches (5cm) in
diameter–slip on a chain, and you're ready
to show off your embroidered pendant.

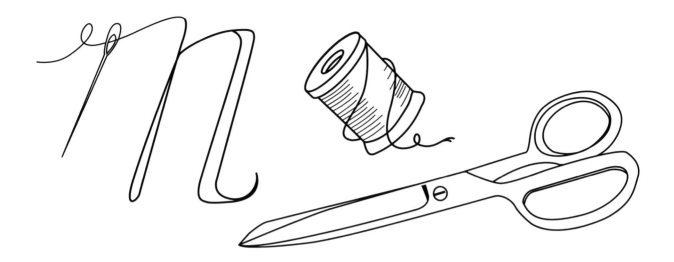

SEWING

From carpenters to chefs, craftspeople hold dear the tools of their trade, and it's no different for stitchers. Emblazon your favorites, from shears to sewing machines to old school wooden spools, on fabric.

▼ SHADE THE STITCHING

A spool of thread makes a fitting motif for pin cushions. Blend short, rather than long, **satin stitches** in different-colored flosses to create shading that looks realistic.

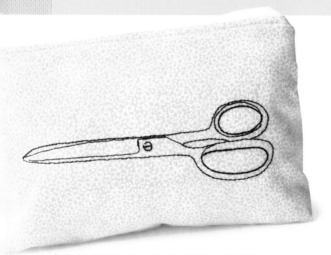

▲ ILLUSTRATE THE CONTENTS

Decorate a pouch with an image showing the sort of items you're storing in it. Scissors detailed in **stem stitch** designate this bag as holding sewing supplies.

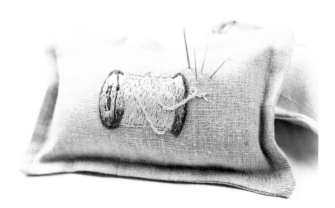

ADD A MONOGRAM

In this motif, the thread in the needle turns into a cursive "N," creating a monogram, but it could have become any letter of the alphabet. Completed in **stem stitch** and **satin stitch,** it graces an apron pocket.

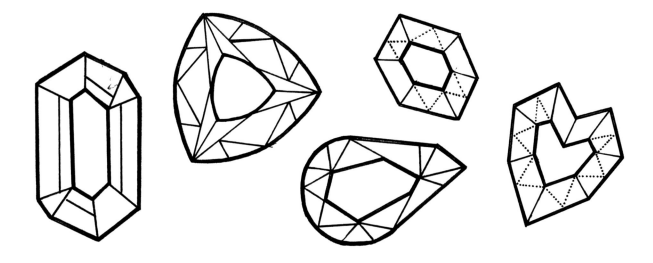

GEMS

Images of cut gemstones have an appealing, geometric simplicity. While they're quick to embroider because they consist of mostly straight lines, they pack a nice visual punch because they look rich and three-dimensional.

▲ STITCH AT DIFFERENT ANGLES

By going in multiple directions, the **satin stitching** reinforces the impression of facets on a cut gemstone, off of which light bounces at various angles. Note how the stitches in the **blanket stitching** are worked in two different lengths to add visual interest.

▼ GO MONOCHROMATIC

Back stitch and **satin stitch** in a shade identical to the foundation fabric. Even when the fabric and thread aren't white, this technique is still called whitework.

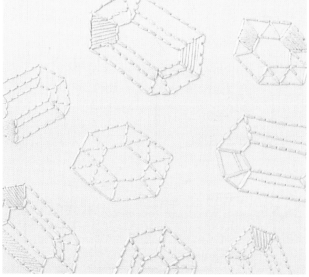

Back the panels with gold paper to hide the stitching.

MAKE EARRINGS

Three successively smaller embroidered cardstock panels link together with jump rings. Stitch them in **back stitch**. Create a subtle shimmer by filling just two or three sections on each one with loosely **satin-stitched** iridescent thread.

ARCHITECTURE

Onion dome churches in Russia, the Taj Mahal, Big Ben, the Leaning Tower of Pisa, the pyramids at Giza—these are just some of the marvels of the world that you might embroider. Or you could look closer to home.

▼ COVER A LID

After embroidering the onion dome church in **satin stitch** with a few **French knot** accents, trim the fabric, wrap it around the lid of an empty jelly jar, and glue to secure. You now have a pretty storage container.

▲ MIX THREAD WEIGHTS

Work the **back-stitched** outline of the church with six strands of floss. Keeping the same thread on your needle, **satin stitch** the windows. Then switch to a single strand of floss to **back stitch** the interior details on this journal cover.

MIX FLOSS & PAINT
Embroider the outline of the image with cotton floss and yarn first,
using a combination of **back stitch**, **couching**, and **satin stitch**.
Then fill some of the areas with acrylic paint. Don't worry if you
accidentally get some paint on the floss. After the pigment dries,
you can cover any problem spots with more stitching.

STITCH A HOUSE

Embroider an image of a friend or family member's home. It makes a unique gift for a housewarming or other occasion, and your loved one will surely treasure it.

What you'll need

Digital or printed image of a house
Pen
Blank sheet of paper
Fabric
Embroidery hoop
Needle and floss
Embroidery scissors

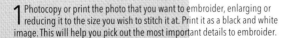

1 Photocopy or print the photo that you want to embroider, enlarging or reducing it to the size you wish to stitch it at. Print it as a black and white image. This will help you pick out the most important details to embroider.

2 Working directly on the printout, draw over the primary and secondary lines. Primary lines consist of all the architectural details of the house–exterior walls, roof lines, windows, doors, columns, and steps. Secondary lines include trees, bushes, and plants. Leave out driveways, sidewalks, and outbuildings.

4 Use any method to transfer the motif onto the fabric, then embroider the design. Here you see **back stitch** for the house and trees, and **link stitch** for the leaves.

3 Place the printout face up on a work surface. Put the blank sheet of paper on it, and trace the lines drawn in step 2. If you can't see through the paper, use the window method instead.

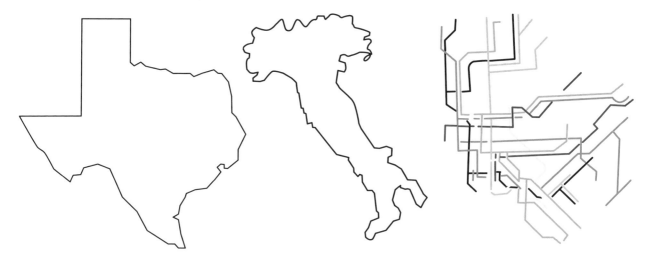

MAPS

Maps can memorialize a special place. You might embroider the outline of a nation or state, a route from one place to another to symbolize a journey, or the path of heavenly bodies.

▲ STITCH A POSTCARD

Have you found a cool vintage postcard that ties to a specific place? Outline that state or country on it in **running stitch**.

▼ USE FLAG COLORS

Fill the outline of a country with **satin stitch**, using the colors of its flag. The simpler the flag and the more recognizable the shape of the nation, the more effective and recognizable the end result.

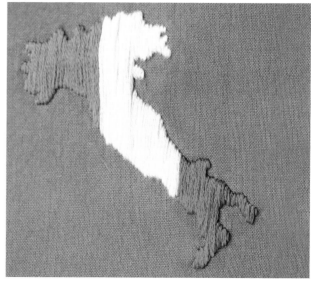

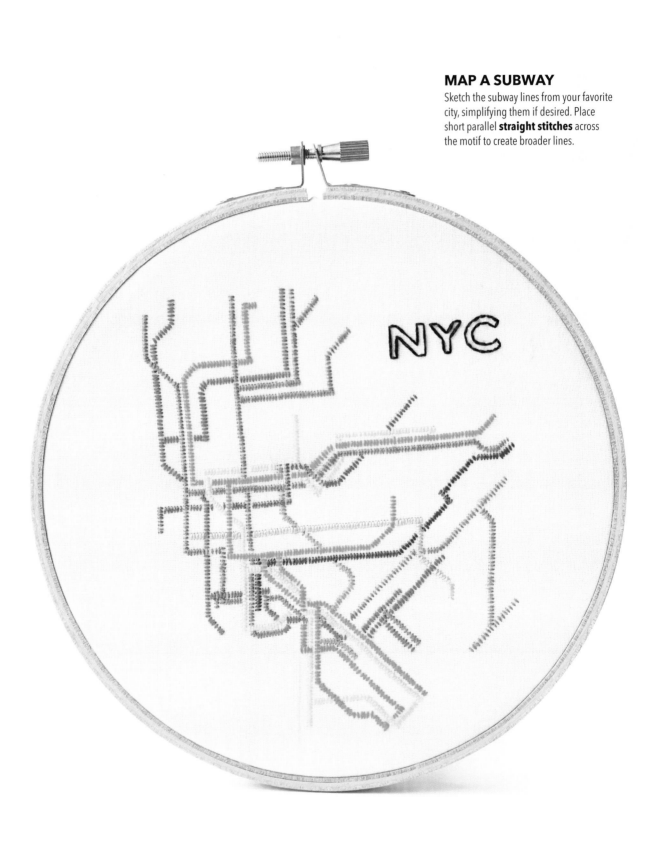

Sketch the subway lines from your favorite city, simplifying them if desired. Place short parallel **straight stitches** across the motif to create broader lines.

PATTERNS

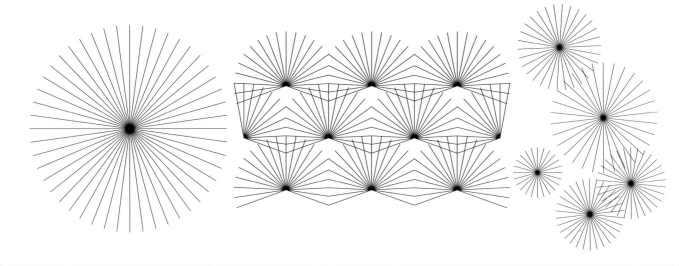

RADIAL

A simple motif of spokes becomes very visually interesting when duplicated, either in the same size or in a mix of diameters. You can work this motif in straight stitches, making it quick to complete.

▲ KEEP THE PALETTE SIMPLE

With a complex motif, keeping the colors to a minimum can really help the embroidery shine. Worked in **chain stitch**, this embroidery sticks to silver and a blue that's slightly darker than the toss pillow.

▼ DECORATE A COLLAR

A Peter Pan collar gets a Japanese treatment with a sun-disc motif reminiscent of that country's flag, but worked up in pastels in a palette drawn from a kimono fabric. The **straight stitches** radiating from the center of each motif are all the same length, with a halo of additional **straight stitches** around them.

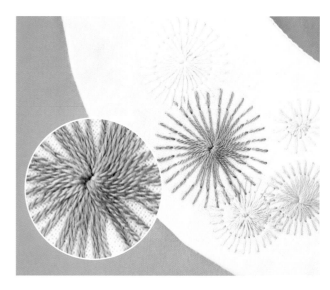

USE VARIEGATED FLOSS

This motif already has plenty of visual interest on its own, but creating it with a variegated floss gives it additional depth and texture, making it more compelling. Worked in **straight stitch**, to quickly add oomph to a notebook cover.

DECO

You can turn any simple motif into something far more complex and visually compelling. The three motifs above derive from the one at far left. It's simply been multiplied, rotated, added to, cropped, resized, and rearranged.

▼ ALTER THE MOTIF

Because the leather cuff was longer than the motif, the right end of the diamond (stitched in pale blue using **running stitch**) was repeated three times. Elsewhere, the points at top and bottom were left out because the cuff was too narrow and they didn't fit onto it.

▲ MIX YOUR STITCHES

This long motif was stitched along the edge of a foldover clutch. The diamonds at the center, worked in **satin stitch**, have a substantial presence that contrasts with the rays around them in a lightweight **running stitch**. The **chain stitching** at the top and bottom frames the design with a heavy border.

STITCH ON WOOD

Make thin plywood brooches using a technique similar to working with paper: Drill at the ends of all lines, gently sand the holes to prevent snagging floss, then stitch the design using two strands of crochet thread and long **straight stitches**. Finally, glue on a pinback.

Felt glued to the back of the brooch gives a neat appearance.

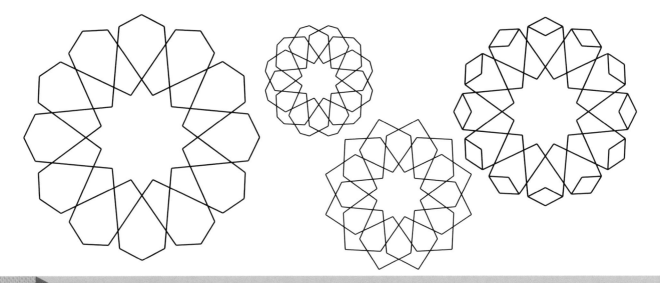

GEOMETRIC

Geometric patterns grab attention because they're strong, with bold, striking shapes. These motifs are orderly, symmetrical, and completely balanced–quite meditative and appealing.

▲ REPEAT THE MOTIF

Place a trio of motifs on a paper card, all aligned with the edge of the paper and all the same size to create a serene composition. On each of these three cards, the star inside the central design is stitched in a lighter color.

▼ USE ONE STRAND

To ensure the **straight stitching** on this notebook cover looks delicate, replace your single strand of cotton floss with a new one the moment it starts looking fuzzy.

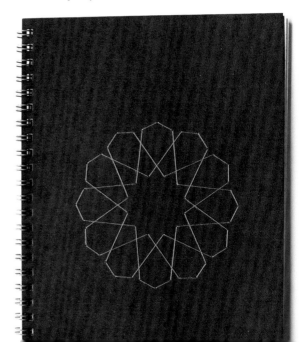

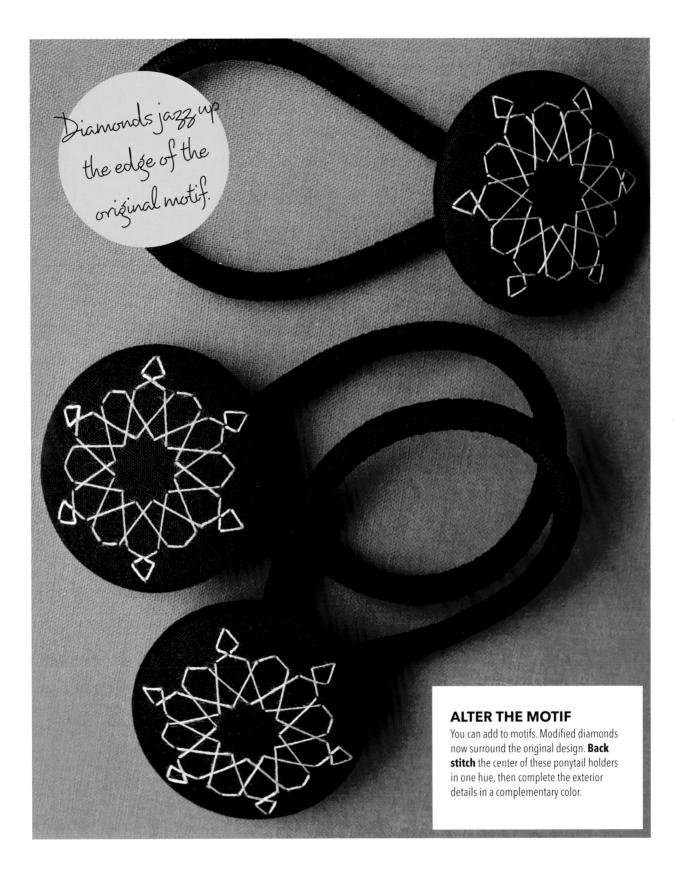

Diamonds jazz up the edge of the original motif.

ALTER THE MOTIF

You can add to motifs. Modified diamonds now surround the original design. **Back stitch** the center of these ponytail holders in one hue, then complete the exterior details in a complementary color.

LINE ART

Lines are simpler to follow than curves, and they embroider up faster because you can make longer stitches–which means stitching fewer of them! Quick and easy–what's not to like?

MAKE LONG STRAIGHT STITCHES

With yarn, you'll make a piece of art fast. The large diameter of the fiber allows you to create designs that are visible from a distance with a bare minimum of extra-long **straight stitches**. This lets you produce even large-scale designs quickly.

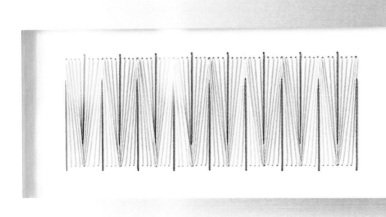

CHOP IT UP

You only need a quarter of the sunburst motif on the opposite page to mimic the sun shining over the mountains. Embellish an old photograph with an extra-large halo of sunbeams and embroider the design in **straight stitches**.

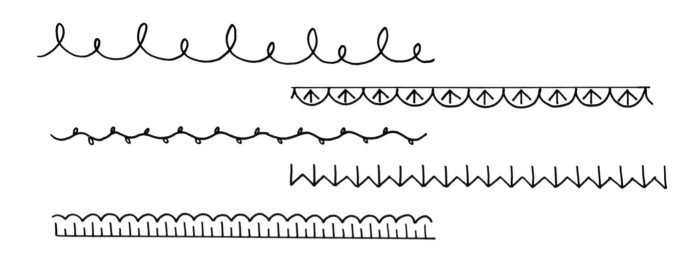

SIMPLE BORDERS

Stitching simple border motifs is meditative, as you keep repeating the design and get into a groove. The edge isn't the only place for a border. Consider running it anywhere down the middle of the fabric.

▼ ENLARGE THE MOTIF

A combination of yarn and **running stitch** makes the gigantic motif along the bottom of a striped shower curtain faster to embroider. When the motif crosses stripes, the color of the yarn changes so it remains visible against the background fabric.

USE HEAVY THREAD

The fabric of this skirt is fairly stiff, making heavy perle floss a good choice to use on it. **Back stitching** traces a playful motif along the flouncy hem.

COMPLEX BORDERS

The repetition in these border designs produces a mesmerizing effect, both to you, as you embroider them, and to the viewer who eventually sees the finished object. You can stitch long sections of them, or just a short area.

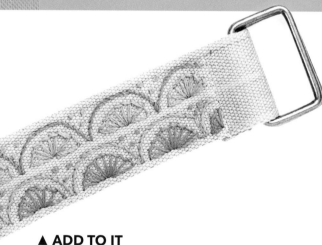

▼ DOUBLE THE DESIGN

Because this café curtain is long, a single row of the border motif didn't feel like enough, so a second section was added atop it. This sashiko design is stitched in the traditional **running stitch**.

▲ ADD TO IT

This is the same motif as the one shown in the photo to the right, but it's completely transformed by the addition of lines and dots. The rugged canvas belting requires a heavy thread to be visible, so embroider with two strands of crewel wool. The areas that look like spokes are worked in a modified **blanket stitch**. There's also **stem stitch** and **French knots**.

SPLASH SOME COLOR

The motif in this photo is the same as in the two pictured opposite, but embroidering it in **satin stitch** on a knit scarf without a stabilizer backing has subtly altered some of its curves. Most of the border is worked in blues, but a pair of semicircles break the pattern and are embroidered in two shades of a complementary color–orange.

SASHIKO

The name of this traditional Japanese technique, originally used by peasants for reinforcing and mending fabrics, translates as "little stabs."

The repeating, interlocking, geometric patterns of sashiko also held together layers of quilting, for warmth and absorbency. Sashiko was usually stitched in off-white thread on indigo fabric, but you can certainly buck tradition. Here are a few pointers.

- Use a sashiko needle. This longer tool allows you to take more stitches at a time, which helps keep stitches the same length.

- Stick to medium-weight fabrics. Tight weaves are hard to pierce.

- If you're right-handed, work right to left, and vice versa.

- Look for commercial templates and trace the design on the right side of the fabric.

Take several stitches at a time on your needle, trying to keep them a uniform length of between ⅛ and ¼ inch (3 and 6mm). The stitches should be only slightly longer than the gaps between them. Once you have several stitches on your needle, pull the thread through and smooth the fabric so it doesn't pucker.

◀ A denim jacket offers a large enough canvas to place different sashiko motifs in various areas.

▼ Making a set of mismatched coasters allows you to try stitching a number of different sashiko motifs without getting into a complex, time-consuming project.

INTERSECT THE LINES CORRECTLY

Sashiko has very specific traditions about how intersecting lines should look from the front. Follow these rules.

Right

Wrong

Corner should meet with a tiny space between

Crossing lines have a space in the middle

Lines should intersect at spaces, not against a stitch

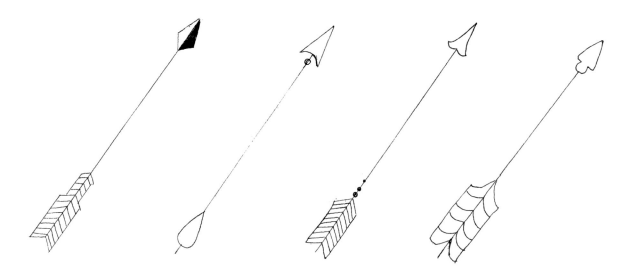

ARROWS

Arrows symbolize all sorts of things: moving toward a goal, strength, courage. Crossed arrows signify friendship. Some people consider them a protective charm against harm. Stitch them solo or in multiples.

▼ SHORTEN IT

Rebrand your high tops by covering the original patch advertising the brand name on the ankle with a way better patch of your own. Cut down the arrow shaft radically so it fits the space.

► INSERT WORDS

Choose a word or phrase that relates to the motif, and add it in. Stitch the entire design in the same color to help wed the writing to the image. Complete it in a mix of **French knots**, **satin stitch**, **straight stitch**, and **stem stitch**.

USE MULTIPLE MOTIFS

Stitch a design and mount it on a picture mat to frame a print of a favorite photo. First embroider each trio of arrows in a mix of **stem stitch**, **back stitch**, **satin stitch**, **couching**, and **French knots**. Then use double-stick tape to attach the fabric to a picture mat. As you do, you'll need to apply the tape first to the front, then to the inside edges of the opening, and finally to the back of the mat board.

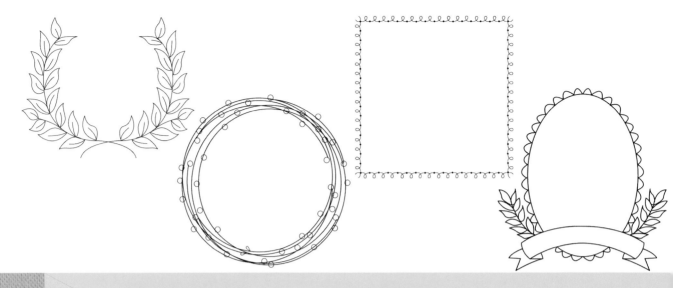

FRAMES & WREATHS

These versatile designs call attention to whatever's stitched inside them while enhancing it still further. The motifs can be sized to fit anything you wish to place inside.

▲ MONOGRAM IT

Embellish a vintage-looking laurel wreath with a letter (or two or three) symbolizing the initials of a favorite person. The color palette consists of sea green with red details for the wreath, and it's reversed for the letter–red with sea green details.

▼ SIMPLIFY IT

The simple **back-stitched** oval frame–minus the banner and laurels–surrounds a silhouette cut from black felt. Note the hoop painted black. A minimal color palette gives this wall art more impact.

July 6, 2013

COMMEMORATE THE DATE

Your wedding day, a special someone's birthday, or a wacky holiday you don't want to forget—enshrine it in the center of a floral wreath. Make each flower with a **French knot** surrounded by **straight stitches**.

► FOLKLORIC

Folk motifs play a huge part in embroidery tradition, from Ukrainian cross-stitched peasant shirts to Mexican dresses, and from the crewel chain-stitched rugs of India to suzani boots.

▼ USE RIOTOUS COLOR

This cup cozy, held shut with a button and elastic, includes eight shades of perle cotton and four of appliquéd felt. The stitching looks complex, but only because it blankets the entire surface. It consists of simple **fly stitch**, **French knots**, **link stitches**, and **blanket stitch**.

▲ ADD LAYERS

Besides **French knots**, **herringbone stitch**, **link stitch**, and **straight stitch**, this bullet-shaped pin cushion has multiple layers of decoration. The scalloped band of white felt is held on to the peach felt with fusible web and tiny straight stitches, and a playful strip of ricrac dances along the bottom.

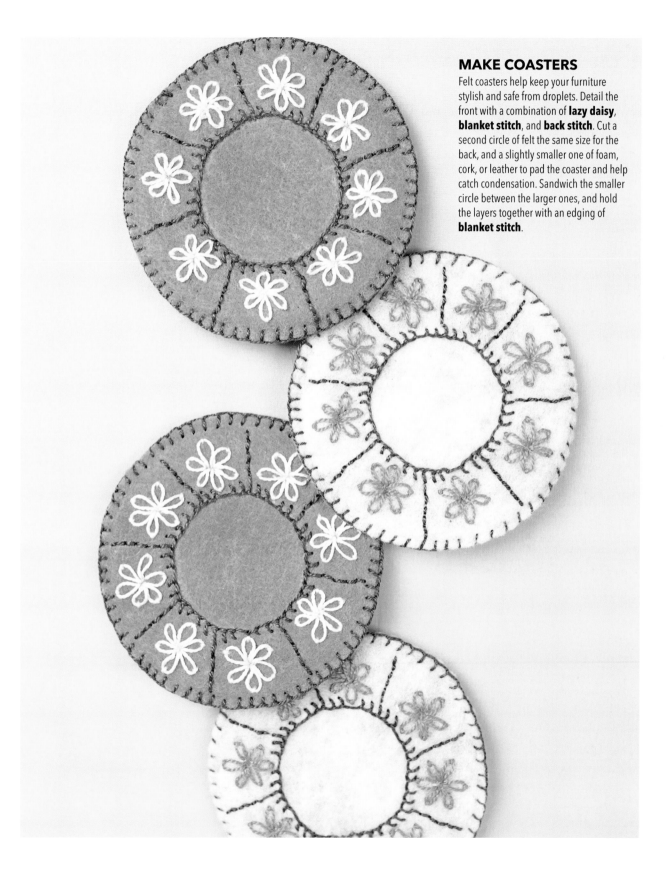

MAKE COASTERS

Felt coasters help keep your furniture stylish and safe from droplets. Detail the front with a combination of **lazy daisy**, **blanket stitch**, and **back stitch**. Cut a second circle of felt the same size for the back, and a slightly smaller one of foam, cork, or leather to pad the coaster and help catch condensation. Sandwich the smaller circle between the larger ones, and hold the layers together with an edging of **blanket stitch**.

CONTRIBUTORS

LUCY BARTER (PAGES 68–69, 76–77, 116–117)
Lucy holds a BA Honors in fashion design and spent several years designing for established children's labels in the UK and US. She discovered the Royal School of Needlework (RSN) and was drawn to its traditional hand-embroidery methods. Her love of needlework inspired her to enroll in the RSN's three-year apprenticeship. After graduating in August 2006, Lucy moved to San Francisco where she taught for the RSN for many years, while also running her own business, Forever Embroidery Studio. In 2015, Lucy co-founded San Francisco School of Needlework and Design, where she also teaches and encourages all to try embroidery and different needlework techniques.
sfsnad.org
Email: lucy@sfsnad.org

JO BUTCHER (PAGES 78–79)
Jo is an embroidery artist with a background in fashion design who creates intricately stitched artworks inspired by classic English country gardens and the rural simplicity of wildflower meadows. After the loss of her first child, she found a need to express herself creatively and discovered the art of traditional embroidery. Recalling stitches learned at school and teaching herself new ones, she began to create her own style. From her home in Somerset, England, she produces delicate embroideries on hand-painted backgrounds and linens. Impassioned by a love of the British countryside and vintage textiles embellished by her grandmother's generation, Jo captures the essence of these influences in her work.
jobutcher.co.uk
Twitter: @sewjobutcher
Email: sewjobutcher@gmail.com

ROBIN AMY DARLING (PAGES 36–37, 80–81, 96–97)
A largely self-taught artist and maker, Robin (aka ShinyFabulousDarling) is a tea-drinking magpie who spends an almost unhealthy portion of her time making pretty pictures with needles. With an inherited love of sparkly things, she lives and works in the northwest of England with one fluffy, cross-eyed cat and an ever-expanding fabric stash. Easily distracted by the next project, she considers herself a professional dabbler in many disciplines, all of them taking up far too much space. Her current obsessions include outlandish ideas, shiny insects, Escher-style fantasy geometry, and stumpwork embroidery.
etsy.com/uk/shop/ShinyFabulousDarling
instagram.com/shinyfabulousdarling
tumblr.com/blog/shinyfabulousdarling

NICK DEFORD (PAGES 40–41)
Nick is an artist, educator, and arts administrator who resides in Knoxville, Tennessee. His work explores the visual culture of cartography, occult imagery, game boards, geographical souvenirs, and other structures of information that is altered to examine the relationship of identity, space, and place. He received his MFA from Arizona State University, and an MS and BFA from the University of Tennessee. He exhibits nationally, with exhibitions at Coastal Carolina University, the Houston Center for Contemporary Craft, University of Mississippi, Lindenwood University, and the William King Museum of Art. He has had artwork or writing published in *Surface Design Journal*, *Elephant* magazine, *Hayden's Ferry Review,* and *Willow Springs*. Currently, Nick is the program director at Arrowmont School of Arts and Crafts in Tennessee. He works on his fiber art practice from his home studio.

CAT EVANS (PAGES 48–49, 54–55, 58–59)
An American raised overseas in a foreign service family, Cat was always exposed by her parents to everything in their host country's culture. So she grew to admire not just art but also the many different aspects of other cultures often viewed as strange and different by outsiders. Always experimenting with different mediums, colors, and designs, Cat re-creates the images that caught her attention as a child—or at least how she remembers them. Embroidery was her mother's hobby, and Cat and her sister learned to stitch at a relatively young age. Fond memories of creating designs and stitching with the women of her family encouraged Cat to embroider again after the birth of her twin boys. Embroidery quickly became her medium of choice, a form of meditation—a way to temporarily escape the world, focus on nothing but the next stitch, and get her creative out.
etsy.com/shop/TwoMushrooms

VALERIE EVANS (PAGES 102–103)
Valerie is known for the tiny embroidered flowers and vintage lace that adorn her embroidered necklaces. The married stay-at-home mom of two started Plaid Love Threads in 2014 after rediscovering the exciting world of embroidery. Although a lifelong California native, she yearns to travel the globe with her husband, collecting souvenir thimbles along the way, and eventually retiring to the English countryside.
etsy.com/shop/plaidlovethreads
instagram.com/plaidlovethreads

LINDA FOERSTER (PAGES 44–45, 92–93)
Linda is a craft artisan who has sewn, embroidered, and crafted since the age of five. She studied art in college but thereafter entered the corporate world; however, she continued her passion for embroidery by doing needlework every evening. When children came along, she took up quilting and used her love of quilting to teach the craft at night in local quilt shops and adult ed for many years. When she took early retirement from corporate life in 2012, her dream was to open a shop on Etsy, which she did in 2013–Holly Creek Home. She decided to revisit her first love– embroidery–and began hand-embroidering pillow covers. Her shop took off from there. Her passion for needlework has turned into a full-time occupation!

SAM P. GIBSON (PAGES 38–39, 46–47)
Sam is an English embroiderer who works in her studio above a recently reinstated Victorian brewery. She produces typographical and decorative embroideries as well as jewelry pieces. Sam was taught to sew by her mother and still uses the sewing box she received as a Christmas gift in 1976. She's influenced by architectural and interior design, Victorian taxidermy and old scientific text and equipment, found photos, pop culture, and modern art. In recent years, she has worked on large, abstract embroidered "paintings" largely based around process: the repetitive arduous nature of a large hand-embroidered task. Though they're usually monochromatic, Sam plans to incorporate more color and graphic form into them.
mrsgibson.co.uk
Email: sam@mrsgibson.co.uk

BECKY JORGENSEN (PAGES 100–101)
Becky is a quilter and pattern designer; her love of the needle started with an embroidery sampler at age eight. She's not afraid to think outside of the box and explore new quilting techniques and ideas. In 2014 she launched the International Association of Quilters–allowing her to share her passions with quilters from around the world and build an active community. Helping others track projects, supplies, ideas, and progress is something she enjoys, so she has designed and sells the *Patchwork Planner & Journal*. Her patterns have appeared in *Thermoweb*, *Andover Fabrics*, *Moda Bake Shop*, *Checkers Dist*, *Primitive Quilts Magazine*, *Fat Quarterly*, and more. You can keep up with the latest happenings, planner pages, and patterns on her blog.
patchworkposse.com

AMY KAROL (PAGES 50–51, 98–99)
Amy makes stuff. She writes books, draws, paints, cooks, teaches crafting classes online, sews, parents young children, tries to exercise regularly, and uses her creativity to both express herself and to engage with her fellow humans. She has had the pleasure of writing two sewing books, *Bend-the-Rules Sewing*, currently in its fourth printing, and *Bend the Rules with Fabric*. She has contributed to quite a few other titles. She currently teaches video classes in a variety of crafts on creativebug. She also sells custom artwork and a natural skincare line in her shop.
etsy.com/shop/amykarol

SALAH KASMO AND LANA TAHA (PAGES 110-111)

Salah and Lana are a couple from Aleppo, Syria. They have lived in the Tokyo area for more than seven years. Salah earned his PhD in industrial engineering from Tokyo Tech, and Lana got her degree in architectural engineering from Aleppo Uni. After being in Japan for so long, they wanted a way to communicate with Japanese society, and then the globe, via a unique international language. At the same time, their Muslim religion urges them to get to know and interact with other cultures. With these grounds, and after careful research, they introduced Islamic geometric art on different applications than the original ones by employing embroidery on paper. This art combines engineering and art in a beautiful way.
facebook.com/circleandlines
etsy.com/shop/circleandlines
Email: circleandlines@gmail.com

ANNALEE LEVIN (PAGES 90-91)

Annalee is a visual artist who works in sculpture, video, and textiles. She's passionate about traditional craft and its potential for application to modern themes and contexts. In recent years, hand embroidery has become central to her art practice. Annalee received a BA in studio art from Macalester College, and an MFA from the sculpture department at the School of the Art Institute of Chicago. She's a graduate of the Royal School of Needlework's Future Tutor Programme, where she spent three years studying hand embroidery. She's based in San Francisco and has taught at San Francisco School of Needlework and Design since its founding in 2015.

SARAH MILLIGAN (PAGES 64-65, 114-115)

Sarah Milligan is a self-taught hand embroidery designer living on the west coast of Canada. She believes anything is better with embroidery on it. Sarah designs embroidery kits and patterns for her line, I Heart Stitch Art, and takes great joy in encouraging others to work more creativity into their lives.

SARA PASTRANA (PAGES 106-109, 112-113)

Sara is a graphic designer who runs a one-woman shop called Gracy Design and Craft. She's a self-taught embroidery artist and a new enthusiast in woodworking and desktop CNC fabrication. The main focus of Gracy Design and Craft is to explore the art of embroidery, a craft that has been associated with antiquated "granny" designs. Sara reimagines traditional stitching techniques and materials into contemporary designs that are stitched onto nontraditional embroidery materials like wood and paper. She lives in Los Angeles, California, with her gorgeous son, Oisin, and caring mother, Gracy.
gracydesignandcraft.com
sarapastrana.com
instagram.com/GracyDesignAndCraft

ANASTACIA POSTEMA (PAGES 60-61, 84-85)

Anastacia is a self-taught embroidery artist from Portland, Oregon. She's good at studying and observing people, and her art is influenced by exploring human emotion. She's inspired by interesting faces, animals, and dreams. Anastacia likes to combine all of these elements into unique designs that she makes into embroidery patterns and kits and sells online and in local shops. When she isn't working on new embroidery designs, sewing, drawing, or teaching elementary students, she enjoys spending time with her husband and two little boys.
etsy.com/shop/oddanastitch
instagram.com/oddanastitch
Email: oddanastitch@gmail.com

ANGELA SALISBURY (PAGES 118-119)

Angela is an embroidery artist in Brooklyn, New York. While living in Tokyo, she learned sashiko from a group of *genki* grandmothers, who taught her to stitch straight and laugh loudly. Her embroidery lives on the Internet at SakePuppets.com, the site she started in 2010 to detail her handcraft discoveries in Japan. Angela's work has been featured by Better Homes & Gardens, The Japan Times, and Design*Sponge, and she co-wrote the book *Tokyo Craft Guide*. Angela works at The Metropolitan Museum of Art and plays roller derby with Gotham Girls Roller Derby. She receives most of her injuries from embroidery.

JEN SEGREST (PAGES 124-125)

Jen is a graphic and web designer from the Dayton, Ohio, area. She loves mid-century modern design, medieval history and art, and traditional hand crafts–her own crafts inevitably get dog hair embedded in them.

RUTH SINGER (PAGES 88-89)

Ruth is a UK-based textile artist specializing in creating artworks with a narrative. She has worked on projects inspired by images of Victorian women criminals, the history of a century-old hospital, and her own gardening grandfather. She creates work for exhibitions and commissions alongside community projects and artist residencies, and had a solo show called *Narrative Threads* in 2015. In 2016 she won the Fine Art Quilt Masters competition at the Festival of Quilts. She's currently artist in residence at the Genetics Department of Leicester University. Ruth has written three books on sewing–*The Sewing Bible, Sew Eco,* and *Fabric Manipulation*–and has created unique projects for books and magazines for many years. She teaches textile workshops and creative retreats in the UK and beyond.
ruthsinger.com
facebook.com/ruthsingertextiles
instagram.com/ruthsingertextiles

LIZ STIGLETS (PAGES 52-53, 122-123)

Liz is the owner/maker of cozyblue, a line of embroidery kits and patterns that make stitching fun and easy. A self-taught illustrator and designer with a focus on modern hand embroidery, she's also mama to two children and a musician's wife. She believes that expressing ourselves creatively is vital to happiness, and her business is all about using embroidery to tap into that creativity. Liz's mission is to encourage everyone to slow down, get cozy, and get crafty. She loves teaching and connecting through her craft.
cozybluehandmade.com
instagram.com/cozyblue
Pinterest: @cozyblue

LINDSAY SWEARINGEN (PAGES 62-63, 66-67, 74-75)

Lindsay is a self-taught fiber artist residing in Northern California. She began embroidery as a form of self care after long stressful days at her job. Since then, she's grown her love of stitching into a small side business, making embroidered hoops and patches. Lindsay loves to use vintage embroidery hoops in her work, and scours eBay daily for new-to-her treasures. She lives with a long-legged monster named Little Brother, who looks a lot like a tuxedo cat.

MARY OWENS WHITE (PAGES 82-83, 94-95)

A simple kit of floss, fabric, needle, and scissors are what Mary calls the tools of her trade. Learning the skill of embroidery from her mother, an artist and painter, Mary was encouraged to paint with thread as a child. Over the course of her life, she has studied fine art, print making, and jewelry making. It is, however, the fine line of embroidery thread and tiny stitches that tie her back to her roots. Mary derives inspiration from nature, the sky, flora, and fauna. Her newest passion is denim embroidery designs and appliqués.
Etsy.com/shop/Marysdreamstudio
facebook.com/marysdreamstudio
instagram.com/marysdreamstudio
Email: Marysdreamstudio@gmail.com

ABOUT THE AUTHOR

Nathalie Mornu created her first piece of embroidery more than 10 years ago. She has written and edited craft books since 2003 and is the author of the best-selling *A Is for Apron.* Her other titles include *Knit & Wrap, Quilt It with Wool, Contemporary Bead & Wire Jewelry,* and *Leather Jewelry.* She stitched the embroidered pieces on pages 42-43 and 120-121.
www.instagram.com/nathaliemornu_embroidery

Publisher Mike Sanders
Associate Publisher Billy Fields
Editor Nathalie Mornu
Design and Art Direction Rebecca Batchelor
Photographer Rebecca Batchelor
Prepress Technician Brian Massey
Proofreader Laura Caddell

First American Edition, 2017
Published in the United States by DK Publishing
6081 E. 82nd Street, Indianapolis, Indiana 46250

Copyright © 2017 Dorling Kindersley Limited

A Penguin Random House Company

18 19 20 10 9 8 7 6 5 4 3 2

002–306712–September/2017

Published in the United States by Dorling Kindersley
Limited

ISBN: 9781465464859
Library of Congress Catalog Card Number: 2017933232

Printed and bound in Canada

All images © Dorling Kindersley Limited
For further information see: www.dkimages.com

A WORLD OF IDEAS:
SEE ALL THERE IS TO KNOW
www.dk.com